NEW & UPDATED!

AN UPDATED PRACTICAL GUIDE TO

THE PUPIL PREMIUM

MARC ROWLAND

A JOHN CATT PUBLICATION

First published 2015
by John Catt Educational Ltd,
12 Deben Mill Business Centre, Old Maltings Approach,
Melton, Woodbridge IP12 1BL
Tel: +44 (0) 1394 389850
Fax: +44 (0) 1394 386893
Email: enquiries@johncatt.com
Website: www.johncatt.com

© 2015 Marc Rowland
All rights reserved.

No part of this publication may be reproduced,
stored in a retrieval system, transmitted in any form or by any means,
electronic, mechanical, photocopying, recording, or otherwise,
without the prior permission of the publishers.

Opinions expressed in this publication are those of the contributors
and are not necessarily those of the publishers or the editors.
We cannot accept responsibility for any errors or omissions.

ISBN: 978 1 909717 63 3

Set and designed by Theoria Design Ltd
www.theoriadesign.com

Printed and bound in Great Britain
by Hobbs the Printers Ltd

Contents

About the Author 5
Foreword 7
Introduction 11

Part One
1. Policy Challenges, Practical Challenges 17
2. Complexities and Barriers 19
3. Shallow Learning 23
4. Take Up 24
5. The Department for Education (DfE) and the Pupil Premium . 26
6. Ofsted and the Pupil Premium 28
7. Parents 33
8. Collaboration 36
9. What Does the Evidence Say? 42
10. Early Years Premium 44
11. Teaching Assistants 46
12. What Works For Those With Barriers in the Classroom 49
13. Transition 52
14. Governance 56
15. Active Ingredients – Case Studies 60
16. Special Schools 66
17. Looked After Children (LAC) 71
18. Successful Schools and the Pupil Premium 75
19. Leadership Traits 78

Part Two
20. What Should I Spend my Pupil Premium on? 91
21. Ideas to Magpie 94
22. Sir John Dunford Interview 100

Part Three
23. Pupil Premium Reviews by the National Education Trust 105

Part Four
24. Ofsted Guidance – Analysis and Challenge Tools for Schools ...127

Part Five
25. Acknowledgements.. 139
26. Further Reading..140
27. References 142

About the Author

Marc Rowland is Deputy Director of the National Education Trust. He joined in March 2007, having previously spent five years at Ofsted in a number of project management roles. He works on partnership and relationship development with key stakeholders across the education sector. Marc has led a number of high profile commissions for the Trust, including reviews of the impact of the Pupil Premium in Warwickshire LA and a cross-phase action research project with Sheffield Schools. Marc has spoken widely about the Pupil Premium and worked with a large number of individual schools to maximise the impact of the funding to improve outcomes for disadvantaged learners. His first book, *A Practical Guide to the Pupil Premium* (John Catt Educational) was published in September 2014.

Marc has also edited two key publications for the Trust – *Beyond Show and Tell, Sharing and Learning to Make 'Best' Practices Even Better*[1] and *Special Education for the Next Generation.*[2] Marc is also currently working on a project with Rosendale Primary School on an Education Endowment Foundation funded randomised control trial that focuses the impact of teaching metacognition in 30 primary schools across the country.

Marc was part of the independent panel set up by Minister of State David Laws MP to review professional standards for Teaching

Assistants. Marc has sat on a number of education advisory groups and has been a primary school governor.

Marc has visited over 150 primary, special and secondary schools in researching this book, and spoke to many more teachers and leaders across the country.

Foreword

"A decent provision for the poor is the true test of civilisation."
Samuel Johnson

"A nation's greatness is measured by how it treats its weakest members."
Mahatma Gandhi

Marc Rowland puts this in the modern educational context when he states that "the measure of a successful education system, whether at local or national level, should be how its disadvantaged pupils perform." In this second edition, Marc has substantially re-written the text, bringing it up to date with a great deal of recent evidence of what is working to raise the attainment of disadvantaged children and broadening the base of his evidence to include more examples from secondary schools.

The Pupil Premium arose from a strong political commitment to social mobility and was driven forward by David Laws as Minister of State for Schools in the coalition government (2010-2015). At a time when many other central government budgets were being cut, £2.5 billion was found to support this commitment. Like Marc Rowland, I am passionate about the quality of education for disadvantaged students and I believe that the Pupil Premium is one of the best policies ever to come out of the Department for Education or its predecessor departments. It is significant – revolutionary, perhaps – for a number of reasons.

First, it focuses on individual children, wherever they are at school. Thus, schools in leafy lanes are obliged to give as much attention to the needs of their disadvantaged pupils as schools in the toughest of inner city areas. After all, a majority of poor people do not live in what we would regard as traditionally poor areas.

Second, intelligent accountability is used to hold schools to account for the impact they make with the funding. Pupil Premium accountability is for impact, not for how the money is spent.

Third, this accountability mechanism means that schools have enormous autonomy in how they spend the Pupil Premium and can respond to the needs of individual children.

Fourth, it has spawned a wealth of evidence, not least in the comprehensive toolkit from the Sutton Trust's Education Endowment Foundation, about what works best. The Pupil Premium has acted as a catalyst to many schools using evidence in a way that they have not done previously.

This book will add to the understanding in schools of how other schools are raising the attainment of disadvantaged students through a combination of responding to individual need and an unerring focus on the quality of teaching.

The Pupil Premium provides resources to schools to put into practice their vision of improving the life chances of every young person on their roll, and it plays strongly to the values and moral purpose that bring most teachers into the profession and which certainly underpin the aims and driving force of just about every school leader I have ever met.

This is a book for classroom assistants, teachers, school leaders and governors in every school in England – and beyond – to support their work with disadvantaged young people. The greatest challenge for our generation is to raise substantially the attainment of the disadvantaged, closing the persistent gap with the achievement of more fortunate young people. No previous generation has managed to do this. With the help of this book and all the other available evidence, we can meet this challenge.

John Dunford, National Pupil Premium Champion 2013-2015

Introduction

Over the past three years, I have been fortunate to visit more than 150 schools across the country to discuss and review how they are using the Pupil Premium grant to improve outcomes for disadvantaged learners. In this Practical Guide I have tried to capture the essentials for success in narrowing the gap, and to share some examples of innovation and excellence which will be useful to schools.

At the heart of every successful school, strong leadership of the Pupil Premium underpins that success. The ambitions for the pupils are driven by values, by ambition for the school community. Meeting accountability targets and Ofsted grades are a by-product, not the end goal. Clarity of purpose and clarity of aims are fundamental. Great schools are a cradle for resilient, effective and confident learners regardless of their socio-economic background.

In 2011, the Pupil Premium was introduced by the coalition government. Its aims were twofold: to improve outcomes for disadvantaged learners, and to narrow the attainment gap between them and their more affluent peers.

The Pupil Premium has become a high profile and popular policy helping schools challenge the underperformance of disadvantaged learners. In the 2015-16 financial year, the premium is £1,300 per primary-age pupil, £935 per secondary-age pupil, and £302 for each child taking up the full 570 hours of funded entitlement to early education. This represents considerable sums of money.

Whatever your view on the policy, it has shone a harsh light on the underperformance of the broad range of pupils defined as 'disadvantaged' by the DfE, including those who live chaotic and challenging lives. In our current education system, just over a third of disadvantaged students leave school with what might be considered a basic entitlement, one which will give them real choices about their future. In the three year period to 2014, only 38.7% of disadvantaged learners got at least five A*-C including English and Maths, compared with 65.9% of their peers.

Furthermore, throughout the country there are significant variations in how disadvantaged pupils perform, and in a number of local authorities the educational outlook for disadvantaged children has been extremely poor. The 2014 KS2 and KS4 results illustrate this well. (See Figures 1 and 2.)

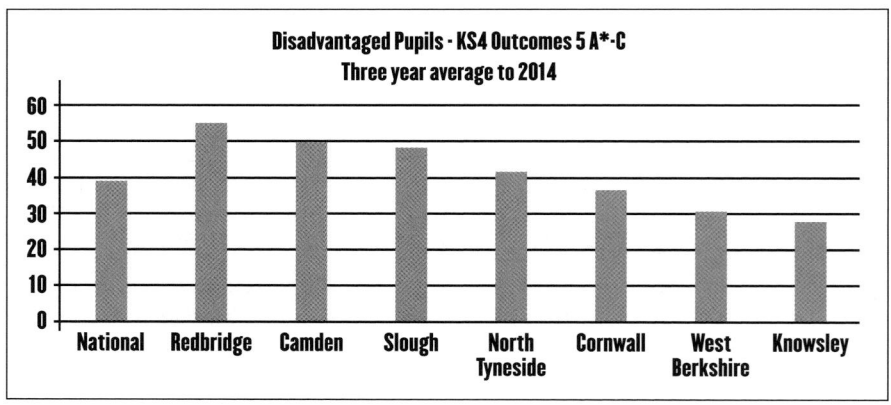

Figure 1: Disadvantaged pupils – KS4 outcomes 5 A*-C three year average to 2014

An Updated Practical Guide to the Pupil Premium

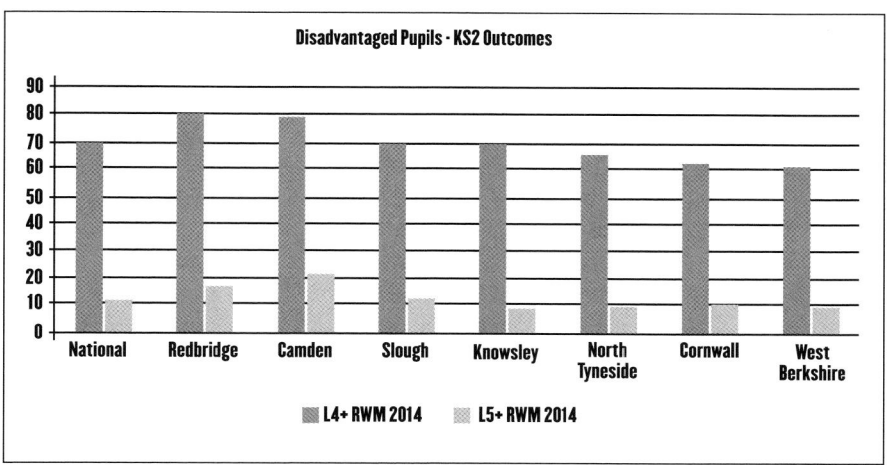

Figure 2: Disadvantaged pupils: KS2 outcomes

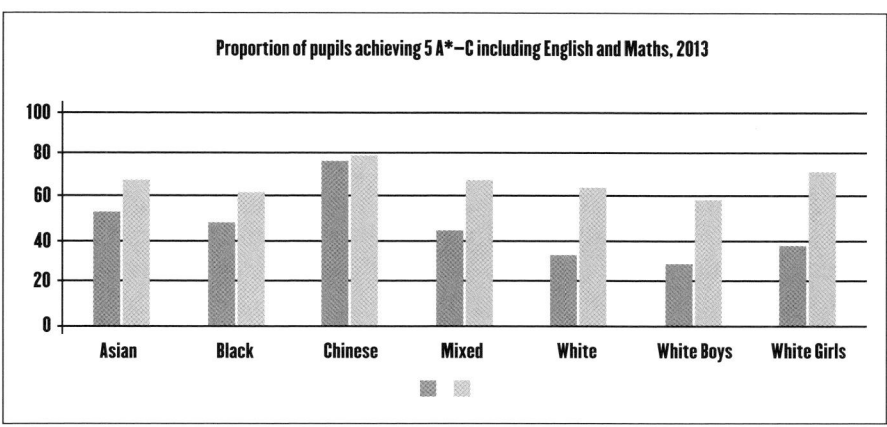

Figure 3: Proportion of pupils achieving 5 A*-C including English and Maths, 2013

Variations are not just simply geographical either. A glance at the outcomes for disadvantaged pupils based on ethnicity shows wide variations in outcomes.[3]

The measure of a successful education system, whether at local or national level, should be how its disadvantaged pupils perform. Further, it is important that we lose the language of 'narrowing the gap'. This may put limits on what pupils can achieve. The focus has to be raising attainment for those from disadvantaged backgrounds if we are to cross the Rubicon. High expectations are crucial.

The primary tool for narrowing gaps is high quality teaching and learning. Poor teaching has a disproportionate effect on disadvantaged learners. The good news is that high quality teaching has a disproportionately positive impact on disadvantaged learners too!

Consistently, the National Education Trust view mirrors that of Andreas Schleicher of the OECD: "our data shows it doesn't matter if you go to a school in Britain, Finland or Japan, students from a privileged background tend to do well everywhere. What really distinguishes education systems is their capacity to deploy resources where they can make the most difference. Your effect as a teacher is a lot bigger for a student who doesn't have a privileged background than for a student who has lots of educational resources."

Put more simply, one of the best measures of an advanced education system is how it treats pupils who are on the margins. How disadvantaged pupils attain has to be the measure of success for an institution. The Pupil Premium can't guarantee complete equality of outcome, but it can give every student in the schooling system the same opportunities to succeed. High quality teaching and learning is fundamental to narrowing the gap. If you don't get teaching and learning right, disadvantage can devour the Pupil Premium like the Atacama devours precipitation.

A note for readers: this Guide refers to National Curriculum Levels which have been at the heart of measuring pupils' progress and attainment in recent years, and these are useful to tell the Pupil Premium story to date. Schools are now properly exploring different ways of recording pupils' progress – 'life beyond levels' – and we at the National Education Trust are working to share best emerging practice in this new era: please visit www.nationaleducationtrust.net.

Marc Rowland

Part One

1. Policy Challenges, Practical Challenges

'Statistics should be used to shine a light, not for a crutch'

'Don't get hung up on the gap!'

Narrowing the attainment gap within the context of an overall raising of standards is the great challenge for our education system. One of the easiest ways to narrow the gap is to have low attainment overall. Clearly though, it is much better for a primary school to have most pupils at L4b+ with a gap, instead of 60% L4b+ for all. The barriers pupils face may be complex and varied. If the focus is on ambitious, excellent outcomes for every individual learner, narrowing the gap is a by-product. Thus, closing the gap through a drop in attainment for non-disadvantaged pupils is not something to celebrate – attainment gaps need to be considered intelligently.

Figure 4 shows a fictitious example that depicts an ideal scenario in terms of data. It is important that schools ask themselves: is this a great place to learn if you come from a disadvantaged background? How do our disadvantaged pupils perform in relation to disadvantaged pupils nationally and locally? How do they fare compared with similar schools. The Education Endowment Foundation's 'Families of Schools' database offers a very useful tool for comparing how pupils are achieving in relation to similar institutions across the country, enabling schools to ask themselves 'is this a great school to go to if you come from a disadvantaged background?' This information is something that should be shared with all school staff. If the key to success for disadvantaged pupils is in the classroom, teachers need to understand how well their pupils are doing compared with other schools. One feature of schools which are struggling with their disadvantaged pupils is that teachers may think that outcomes are as good as they can be, and there is 'no more we can do'.

An Updated Practical Guide to the Pupil Premium

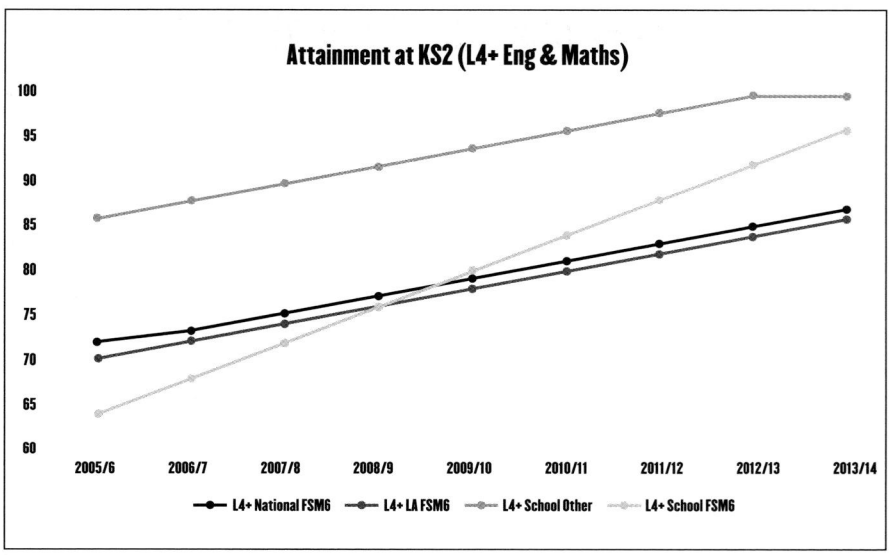

Figure 4: Raising attainment and narrowing the gap

2. Complexities and Barriers

One of the dilemmas many school leaders face is supporting vulnerable pupils who are not eligible for Pupil Premium funding. Juliette Jackson, a headteacher of three schools in Inner London, points out that some of the most vulnerable pupils in her care are those who come from 'minimum wage' families, where parent and carers work long hours, often in shifts, for little money. These families can be both materially poor and time poor. To tackle this problem, many schools have taken a pragmatic approach, providing resources and intervention at the point of need, and ensuring that the Pupil Premium funding is not diverted away from its target audience. This is why focusing on using the funding to improve the quality of teaching and learning should be a priority. Whilst schools are accountable for outcomes for disadvantaged learners, targeting the Pupil Premium on the classroom can have a positive impact on all learners within the 'Ever 6 FSM' category.

Within the 'Ever 6 FSM' category, the barriers to learning can be varied and complex. It is vitally important therefore to tailor Pupil Premium funded activity towards specific pupils, rather than just adopting a broad approach. Schools must set their own vision for their pupils, whether those with special educational needs (SEN), those who have English as an additional language (EAL), or those who are looked after children (LAC).

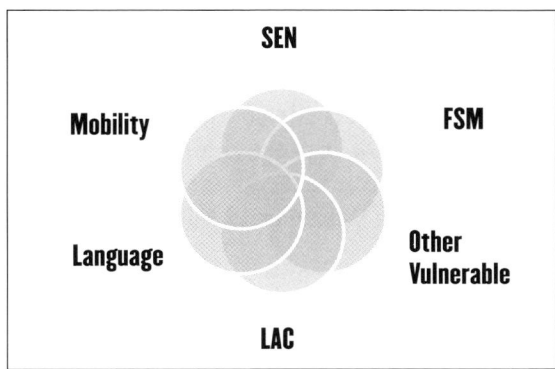

Figure 5: Some of the complexities for disadvantaged learners. Poverty may not be the primary factor preventing higher attainment

It is well worth remembering that some barriers don't come with a label. This is all about knowing children and young people so we can understand them better and help them overcome their challenges. Understanding barriers must not inadvertently create an excuse culture. The best way to raise pupil self-esteem is for them to be successful in the classroom. Extended time away from learning in nurture groups may help in the short term, but it may risk enhancing educational disadvantaged. This is why impact evaluation is crucial.

One headteacher in the North East described a parent who arrived at her school with two children at his side. He announced that his children were coming to 'this school'. He didn't know their names and the children had recently spent various periods in care. Catch-up classes with untrained Teaching Assistants are not going to overcome the challenges that children in these scenarios face. Such circumstances need high quality, tailored support and excellence in the classroom. At the same time we must avoid any sense of 'labelling' learners. The most effective schools have high expectations and high ambitions for every pupil, regardless of background.

Understand Children and Their Families Before Acting

An enthusiastic teacher from a London school put together a superb folder for her Year 5 and 6 children called 'Things to do in London for free'. It was beautifully presented, included all the world class museums and galleries that many London children have close to home. It also included details of free travel and other practical advice. After the school holiday, the teacher did a quick check to see what impact the folder had had. Not one of the 28 disadvantaged children had felt able to use the file. It benefited those children who would have gone anyway.

It is important to understand the barriers to opportunity that children face *before* acting.

There are some other challenges to be wary of too – and these come with a word of warning that they are informed observations, and not from a statistical analysis:

- Many schools with high percentages of Pupil Premium students appear to do better as they have greater spending power, but context can affect this.
- Lower spending capability can mean a greater challenge for small schools and for those with low FSM numbers (for whom the increase in funding will be particularly welcome), though it can still be well spent on staff development and on partnerships with other schools.
- High Special Educational Needs (SEN) numbers within disadvantaged pupils can mean that low attainment is more difficult to shift; in some cases deprivation may not be the main determinate in lower attainment.
- This is also the case for many schools with high levels of children in care and for schools with high mobility. Counter-intuitively, it is not always the newly joined pupils who get stuck, as there is often a sharp focus on them as a vulnerable group. To overcome these challenges, quality teaching and support staff across schools, supported by a personalised approach, becomes even more important.

Roy Blatchford, Director of the National Education Trust, used to give a talk called 'Have you ever met a mugger who's read *Middlemarch*?' The key message is: whatever else we do in schools, think beyond accountability measures and make sure every learner leaves school with the dignity of being literate and numerate as a minimum. This will give young people some choice. At the same time, don't suppress your expectations of those from disadvantaged backgrounds. Seventeen Year 6 children from Grove Primary School in Handsworth, Birmingham secured a grade C in GCSE Maths this year, nine of whom were eligible for the

Pupil Premium. The school has over 60% of pupils from disadvantaged backgrounds, 77% of learners with English as an additional language, and has been securing good GCSE grades in Maths for a decade.

> *'The Pupil Premium has enabled us to ensure that learning is more effectively transferred into life, improving the sustainable impact of the education we offer.'*
>
> Simon Knight, Special School Deputy Headteacher, Oxfordshire

3. Shallow Learning

The National Education Trust recently conducted a mathematics review for a school in the West Midlands. At first glance, the KS2 results look acceptable – nearly 90% L4+; a closer examination of the data showed that only a third of those children are L4b+. Children achieving a L4a have a 95% conversion rate to GCSE C+ in English and mathematics. With children at L4b or L4c that level is 72%. If the focus is solely on the accountability target of L4c, learning is not at the level it needs to be to ensure that children attain well and enhance their life chances. In this particular school, Pupil Premium funding is spent on 'one to one' in Year 6 and on Teaching Assistants.

One might think of this as the difference between organically farmed chickens, reared and nurtured as individuals, and battery hens – repeating the same task in the same place over and over again. The pressures are understandable, but to extend the metaphor just a little further, most of us prefer the idea of free range eggs over battery, even if it is harder work for the farmer, takes longer and is sometimes more expensive to achieve.

This 'shallow learning' approach is akin to filling up on confectionery to run a marathon. A child stumbling or being dragged to a Level 4c at the end of Key Stage 2 is like a refined sugar boost. It's briefly satisfying, but a few hours later there is an inevitable dip in performance.

Similarly, the L4c child, moving into a new learning environment and new learning culture, with outside influences increasingly impacting on their lives, can be lost in the challenging environs of the secondary school and its curriculum. Last minute booster classes to meet accountability measures create shallow learning. Sticking plaster solutions don't work – they fall off. Instead, schools must put into place well-researched, comprehensive, and flexible *long-term* plans if they want to address the fundamental barriers to learning and attainment.

4. Take Up

Many headteachers indicate that a number of pupils in their schools who are eligible for free school meals choose not to claim them, and thus the school does not receive its due funding. A common reason given for this is the social stigma attached to claiming free school meals; some schools find that after the introduction of a cashless system at lunchtime (hiding the identity of those claiming) the number of families applying for free school meals goes up.

One school offers families a 'learning voucher' worth £50 if they sign up for free school meals and another offers free uniform. This incentive is funded by the Premium itself. Another school offers a prize draw to encourage take up. Anyone who fills out a form, eligible or not, is entered to de-stigmatise application.

Non-take up of FSM is a challenge nationally (a DfE report says non-take up by eligible families stands at 11%).[4] Schools need to be proactive in encouraging take up: an increasing number of schools offer families a learning voucher to buy books, uniform or stationery for signing up, with some success. Universal Free School Meals (UFSM) means that primary schools need to be even more forceful in ensuring families 'sign up' and explain that this is about whole school improvement and more than a free lunch.

Anecdotally, there is also a concern, especially because of the requirement to publish information about Pupil Premium funding on the school's website, that the Pupil Premium may create negative feelings between parents, with those not eligible feeling that their children are missing out unfairly. Headteachers have to walk a tightrope. It is crucial that school leaders ensure that all parents know and understand that the Pupil Premium can lead to whole school improvement. No one loses out if the whole class attains well.

There is a strong link to school culture and values here. Talking to parents as well as sending home letters in book bags. Modelling best practice with school website statements (see Stocksbridge Junior School in Sheffield as an exemplar that is updated termly).

Visit the following school websites for good examples of Pupil Premium reports:

Primary: St Eugene de Mazenod Catholic Primary School, Camden
Junior: Stocksbridge Junior School, Sheffield
Special: Carwarden House School, Surrey
Secondary: Baylis Court School, Slough

The DfE has Early Years Premium and Pupil Premium Registration Forms available. Model letters are also available.

5. The Department for Education (DfE) and the Pupil Premium

The consistent and important message from the DfE is encouraging, given some of the concerns school leaders have expressed. The DfE have emphasised that 'the government is quite serious in its ambition not to micromanage schools'; 'schools should be the decision-makers, using evidence to inform professional judgements'. The DfE has no particular view on using the Pupil Premium funding on whole-school initiatives (for example, teacher CPD on improving marking), as long as the attainment gap is closing, within a school context of generally improving attainment.

The DfE acknowledges the importance of pastoral initiatives to enable a child's readiness to learn, and point out that – in part – its national Summer School programme is based on this premise. Equally the Department warns against using the funding as a substitute for social welfare programmes which no longer exist. The clear message is that spending Pupil Premium on pastoral initiatives is fine as long as some thought has gone into how it will improve educational attainment, and how the impact will be measured.

The DfE takes a similar position on enrichment activities. It is important that enrichment activities have some educational goal if they are funded by the Pupil Premium (for example, improved science knowledge, or engagement in lessons). The DfE points out that schools still get a deprivation element in their mainstream dedicated schools grant (DSG), which can be used to subsidise trips that are not educational. Again, robust evaluation and clear success criteria are crucial.

Although the DfE has no pointed view on whole school approaches, if there were a situation where funding could either be spent on a non-FSM child who was underachieving, or an FSM child who was performing well, the funding should still be spent on the FSM child. It stresses that the Pupil Premium funding should not be conceptualised as a 'catch-up' initiative for underperforming students, and that attention and funding should be readily focused on those disadvantaged students who are performing well, to help them do even better.

The Pupil Premium Awards[5]

The awards, run by the Department for Education in partnership with the TES, reward and recognise some of the schools that are doing the most to raise attainment for disadvantaged pupils.

The awards also act to showcase examples of some of the most effective practice which other schools can learn from. Schools can win individual prizes of up to £250,000.

6. Ofsted and the Pupil Premium

There is a concern that accountability measures might drive activity with the Pupil Premium and encourage the 'quick fix', or for schools to want to show they have spent the money on something physical, like iPads or a teaching assistant. However, Ofsted constantly reinforces the DfE's message that it is up to the school to decide how the Pupil Premium is spent, and confirm that there is no prescription about how, but they will make judgements on the impact of Pupil Premium spending. Pupil Premium money can be spent 'where school leaders feel it is most needed'. However, the attainment gap and the impact of the spending are high profile issues for inspectors, and inspectors will want to see four key things:

1. A general trend towards closing the attainment gap within a context of generally improving attainment.
2. All pupils, including those eligible for the Pupil Premium, being tracked and making at least good progress.
3. Robust evaluation of any activity which is funded by the Pupil Premium.
4. Clear justification of why the Pupil Premium has been spent as it has.

Evaluation is not just about proving that something works. It is about understanding impact and the active ingredients for success or where things have gone wrong. (See Table 1.)

Evaluation could include: the impact of short-term academic interventions on pupil attainment; the impact of longer term interventions, such as teacher training, on the quality of teaching or quality of feedback; or, for pastoral activities, parental questionnaires about attitudes to learning. A less robust approach, where schools simply state that 'we send pupils on trips to the theatre,' or 'we spend it on a nurture group led by a teaching assistant', is not good practice.

Inspectors will want to hear what impact the theatre trip had, or what training the teaching assistant received, who was involved, what will the follow up be?

- Focus on impact, on outcomes. This is where you are accountable.
- Be clear about your rationale for spending. Why did you choose to spend your funding in this way?
- Is the Pupil Premium reaching those it was intended for?
- Ask if interventions are linked to what is happening in the classroom.
- Evaluate rigorously – whole group and individual. Be confident when talking (able to talk) about what you've stopped doing, and what you have changed.
- Have high expectations. This is even more important for disadvantaged pupils.

Chris Wood, HMI

'The challenge for any school is to provide learning opportunities of the highest quality for all its pupils. The Pupil Premium has enabled us to create a place of excellence, endeavour and optimism.'

Sam Gaymond, Junior School Headteacher, Sheffield

An Updated Practical Guide to the Pupil Premium

Aim	Boost pupil progress through improved feedback	Evaluation
Actions	Cycle of CPD for staff	Monitor quality of CPD
	Additional time for staff for feedback	Monitor that additional time is being used effectively
Expected impact	Disadvantaged (target) children to make XX months of accelerated progress	Baseline and post-trial discussions with staff and pupils

Table 1: Diagram of simple evaluation

Ofsted recognises the concern raised by headteachers that there are vulnerable students in need of support who are not eligible for Pupil Premium funding, and give a pragmatic spending solution in response to this issue, which remains in line with the DfE's requirement to prioritise Pupil Premium spending on eligible students.

Put simply, if an intervention is required for 100 pupils and, of these, only 60 are eligible for Pupil Premium funding, then 60% could be funded with Pupil Premium money (for accounting purposes), with the remaining 40% being funded by other sources. This allows schools to meet the needs of all the children in their schools, and use the Pupil Premium funding to create economies of scale. Ofsted have highlighted this approach in their second report on the Pupil Premium (The Pupil Premium – How Schools are Spending the Funding Successfully to Maximise Achievement, February 2013).

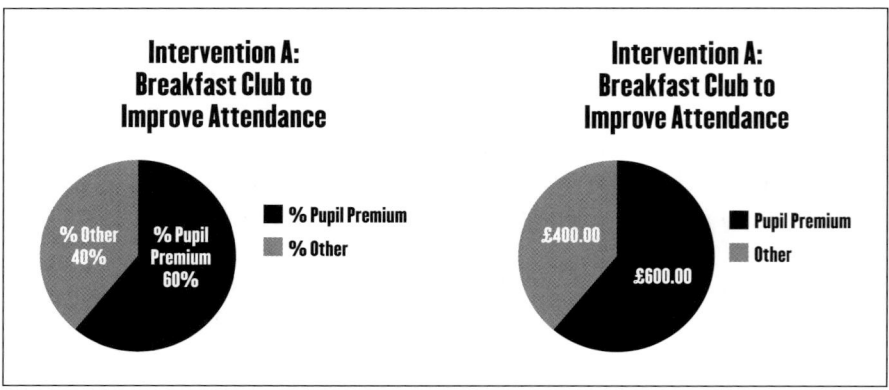

Figure 6: Ensuring Pupil Premium funds are spent on disadvantaged learners

When it comes to Ofsted and the Pupil Premium, leadership of the funding is again crucial. Headteachers need to be able to tell their school's Pupil Premium story when 'An Inspector Calls'. Schools do not want to be like the Birlings, finding it difficult to take responsibility, or to understand or articulate their role in the impact of the funding on pupil outcomes.

Thomas Hepburn Academy in Gateshead have developed a simple model to monitor this (see Table 2). It's not about accounting for every penny against each pupil. It is important to remember that equality of opportunity is not the same as equality of provision.

Pupil	Attainment (date)	Barrier					Activity				Notes
Name		SEND	Poor L/N	Attendance Punctuality	Behaviour	Self Esteem	Feedback	Catch Up N	Catch Up L	Music Club	
RM		ASD					X			X	
SW			L&N	X	X		X	X	X		
WS			N			X	X	X			

Table 2: Pupil Premium provision map

This approach is important because the school recognised that labels such as 'SEND' or 'Pupil Premium' were not enough, and that they needed to dig far deeper to effectively support their pupils.

Many schools are good at describing what they do with the Pupil Premium funding, but fewer can describe what impact it has. Regular tracking where the money is spent and what impact it is having is crucial from an Ofsted perspective, but it also allows for more effective use of the money, as interventions can be tweaked or changed if they are not having the intended impact.

The most successful schools are thorough in their monitoring of every pupil, and thorough in their knowledge of every child. Good schools expect their Year 3 pupils to make the same progress over the year as their Year 6 pupils, so every member of staff feels equally responsible for the end of Key Stage results.

Ofsted have provided three very helpful reports on Pupil Premium which tell a story of improving practice nationally. Links can be found in the 'Further Reading' section at the end of this book.

> *'Through the Pupil Premium our children have benefitted from real life experiences that have positively informed their academic and social learning journeys.'*
>
> Samera Ahmed, Primary Academy Vice Principal, Reading

7. Parents

A key aspect of the Pupil Premium is effective communication with parents. Many colleagues ask about good examples of Pupil Premium statements on websites. It is important to keep things simple. Schools should ask themselves 'who is the message for?' and stick to the core facts: what are you spending the money on, why, and what impact are you expecting? Has it worked? Baylis Court School in Slough, Carwarden House School in Surrey and Stocksbridge Junior School in Sheffield provided excellent examples of this approach (see 'Take Up' section).

> *'We have learnt many valuable lessons over the past few years about disadvantaged students, in particular the need to ensure they receive highly effective teaching and that barriers to attainment are identified on an individual level.'*
>
> Dr Martina Lecky, Secondary Headteacher, London

Rosendale Primary School like all successful schools, focuses its energies on the needs of their pupils and what happens in the classroom to improve outcomes for learners.

The school draws on research (no ability grouping, no homework, offers time for teachers to provide quality feedback and for their own scholarship), understands the need to have the strong foundations for learning in place (attitudes, attendance, listening skills, language development, metacognition), and the blurring of the boundaries between the primary barriers to learning (SEN, deprivation etc).

Its Pupil Premium expenditure is underpinned by relentlessly high quality teaching, and the school teaches with open doors. For example, parents can attend the first 30 minutes of their children's lessons with them every day. During this time, children undertake independent learning tasks or respond to their next steps feedback from teachers. Further, simple innovations that make the most of times when parents are already in school (such as class assemblies) to provide curriculum updates are highly effective. The crucial ingredient is that parental engagement forms a key plank of the school's values, and therefore the school development plan, rather than a tick box exercise.

Its Pupil Premium expenditure is underpinned by relentlessly high quality teaching, and the school teaches with open doors. For example, parents can attend lessons with their children once a week to improve parental involvement and attitudes to learning.

Hammond Academy, an excellent primary in Hemel Hempstead, uses a proportion of its Pupil Premium funding in vouchers for parents. Access to the grant is negotiated through highly skilled, highly committed Parent Partners who help broker appropriate uses of funds which help overcome barriers to learning. Underpinned by excellent teaching and very high expectations, the school focuses on the cultural gap and the engagement gap as a way of breaking down barriers to young people achieving their potential. More information about the school's use of the Pupil Premium can be found at: www.hammondacademy.org.uk/88/pupil-premium.[6]

Another school in North London has an expectation that its teachers are systematically expected to meet and talk with the parents who find engagement with teachers more difficult. These are short discussions, informal discussions in the playground at drop off and pick up where possible. They are part of a process of building relations with parents and carers who may lack confidence. Dame Alison Peacock wisely posed the question – *'is it parents that are hard to reach, or are we a hard to reach school?'*

A Little Bit of Magic… Don't Make Assumptions About People
'A younger sibling had run away from a parent, causing a bit of a fright and the parent reacted by shouting at the child and then swearing, mainly I think due to embarrassment in front of other parents.

The Head asked the parent to come into school to calm down, gave him a cup of tea and staff distracted his children by talking about some books that were on the table in the entrance hall.

A few minutes later, the father picked up a book and began to read it to his two children. He used different voices for different characters and was so engaging that quite a few members of staff were stunned.

The best bit though was that his child's class teacher came forward and not only praised him for such brilliant storytelling, but insisted that he come into school to read to the children. The parent stood taller, his child beamed with pride at him and he left school valued.'

It is so easy to assume that disadvantaged pupils don't get that love of storytelling from their parents but for this family – maybe it's just that they need more wonderful books to take home and share. We always talk about finding children's passion. Maybe that's the key to parental engagement – finding their passion and getting them to share it with the children!

Deputy Headteacher

> *'Aim for parental empowerment, not parental engagement.'*
>
> Rebecca Clark, National Director,
> Oasis Community Learning

8. Collaboration

Partnership working can be a significant weapon in narrowing the gap. The Pupil Premium resource can go even further through the use of economies of scale, especially for schools with fewer disadvantaged students. Genuine partnership like this is all too rare.

Estelle Morris famously challenged Oxfordshire Heads to 'give' their best teacher to the struggling school down the road in the spirit of partnership. That level of collaboration across the country may be some way off, but the notion of sharing is one to be embraced – with a careful understanding about how best to collaborate. As one headteacher observed wryly, "if the children can share a mattress, we should be able to share a maths teacher".

The National Education Trust has been working with a group of schools in a remote rural area. The group includes three isolated primary schools from a series of linked villages. They didn't even share lifts to the CPD session – forget sharing a specialist maths teacher! They do both now, bursting with ambition to make things better. Courage to do things differently is needed by leaders, both headteachers and governors.

How can we ensure that under-performing schools look outwards, develop a culture of restlessness to improve, and are able to learn from others?

Genuine collaboration is vitally important. Without genuine and effective collaboration, the Pupil Premium policy will serve only to enhance gaps, because whilst good schools speed off into the distance, those falling behind will continue to look inwards, doing more of the same and trying to free themselves from regular inspection. If this happens, there is a risk that the Pupil Premium funding itself may be reduced, restricted or even stopped.

Nicola Shipman from the Steel City Partnership of Schools in Sheffield tells a powerful story of school-to-school collaboration within their Multi Academy Trust. Working to a shared vision, three primary schools have undertaken a range of partnership initiatives to narrow gaps for disadvantaged learners. These include a move from 'continual professional development' to 'joint practice development', much of which is focused on lesson study to improve the quality of teaching and team work. Every teacher across the partnership has an individual coaching plan. Action research takes place across the partnership on sharply focused questions such as 'How are Teaching Assistants used?' or 'How has the teaching of history impacted on literacy across schools?'

The schools also use more straightforward techniques to try to improve outcomes. Free breakfast club if children attend on time for ten days in a row has been quite a success!

> One of the best ways to collaborate on approaches to improving outcomes for disadvantaged learners is to take part in an Education Endowment Foundation trial. Sign up for alerts about new projects via their website. Not only does this bring new ideas with regards to the trial, but also wider partnership working beyond LA borders builds knowledge and understanding about effective impact evaluation.

In 2014/15, Sheffield Local Authority ran a collaborative Pupil Premium Action Research Project with ten schools over 18 months. Pam Smith, who led the project said "We were very keen to investigate best practice in schools at regional and national levels, in order to develop our own innovative approaches here in Sheffield. The selection of schools involved reflects a wide and diverse range – seven primaries (including one infant and one junior), geographically spread; two secondaries which are partner schools for at least one each of the primaries; and a special school. Each adds its unique context and, without doubt, it contributed to the generation of a rich bank of expertise and experience. The regular opportunities for colleagues to collaborate on aspects of the project and meet to discuss progress has been integral to the success of the venture. It has given us the chance to share developing practice but also to analyse the challenges schools are facing and discuss possible solutions – including stopping an activity altogether if it wasn't working and trying something different!"

The report is important because Sheffield Local Authority worked over a long period with a group of schools from a range of contexts and at different stages on their improvement journey. One of the schools that took part was Stocksbridge High School. This secondary case study is helpful as it describes the process the school went through and the valuable lessons that go well beyond Pupil Premium – especially in relation to effective ways to improve practice.

The full report, detailing the impact in individual schools and the wider findings from the research can be read on the National Education Trust website.[7]

> **Stocksbridge High School – Number on Roll: 857**
> **Proportion of Disadvantaged Learners: 22%**
> Pupil Premium funding was allocated to a range of additional provisions such as breakfast clubs, catch up intervention and incentives around attendance and punctuality.
>
> While there was some evidence of impact around the particular focus of each intervention, improved progress overall had not been embedded and our gaps in attendance, behaviour and therefore pupil progress, had not narrowed.
>
> In looking at our data and taking lessons from research, we concluded that an 'intervention culture' had grown up which was having the unintended consequence of reducing the sense of accountability that each teacher feels for the progress of students with the most significant barriers to learning. In response to this, we redirected time and money away from additional intervention and toward improving training and systems which support high quality teaching every lesson. We did this through:
>
> - Investment in improved data tracking systems to inform quality assurance and improvement planning.
> - Investment in training and support for our middle leaders in quality improvement strategies, action planning and impact evaluation.
> - Increased investment in professional development for teachers, through:

- use of the Outstanding Teacher Programme and Improving Teacher Programme
- creation of a team of 'lead learners'
- institution of the 'lesson study' approach to self-improvement.

We applied to take part in the Action Research Project as we hoped to learn from others, locally and nationally. We hoped, specifically, that the action research approach would help us to be much more effective in evaluating the impact of our work. We recognised that we had been doing lots of good things with the best of intentions, but in the end we didn't have a clear picture of what had or hadn't worked or why this was the case.

I had been fortunate to be part of some NHS training on the science of 'Quality Improvement' and I had been personally inspired by the evidence of transformational work in many different fields. This project excited me as it was a chance to learn more about how to apply this approach in school.

We began with a 'global aim' for the project. The key here was not to aim at something we were certain we would achieve. Instead we were bold enough to name what we really wanted to achieve, safe in the knowledge that we almost certainly wouldn't! This provided a clear framework within which we could evaluate our success (and failure) and also ensured that we didn't set out simply to find a quick fix for a symptom instead of tackling the underlying causes of the problem.

Global Aim

We believe that a measure of quality in education is the extent to which excellence is achieved by all students, irrespective of disadvantage or barrier to achievement.

Our aim in this project is to eliminate variation in achievement between Pupil Premium students and non-Pupil Premium students through a focus on quality provision, informed by a rigorous cycle of review and planning.

Project Actions
Throughout the project, we chose to track the impact of some of our improvement strategies on our most disadvantaged students:
- Partnership working with Stocksbridge Junior School to implement the use of Kagan structures in order to improve cooperative learning at the High School: by adopting classroom approaches recognised from primary school, we hoped to smooth transition. We also wanted to test the idea that supporting children to be effective cooperative learners would have the most significant impact on the most disadvantaged students.
- Use of attendance panels: as well as a gap in achievement, there was a clear gap in typical levels of attendance between our Pupil Premium and non-Pupil Premium students. Through the project we wanted to evaluate the specific impact of this strategy on our Pupil Premium children.
- Academic mentoring: we introduced a more systematic programme of academic mentoring involving subject teachers and form tutors working with students to develop targets around data collection and reports. Through the Action Research Project we sought to assess the impact of the system on the progress of our Pupil Premium students.

Impact of the Project Actions and Other Learning
We do have a pattern of narrowing gaps between the progress made by Pupil Premium children and others, evident in GCSE outcomes and in the progress tracking data for students in lower years.

Our overall attendance figures improved from 2013 to 2014, though the level of persistent absence amongst Pupil Premium children actually increased as did the gap between this figure and that for other children in the school. It is still too early to reflect on the specific impact of Kagan and indeed on our academic mentoring work.

The most significant impact of the project to date has been the way we now think differently about improvement planning. The action research methodology has found its way into every aspect of our appraisal, quality assurance, planning and review processes.

We have carried out training for senior and middle leaders on the quality improvement approach. I am confident that this change in focus and approach has led to genuine improvement in the quality of teaching which in turn has resulted in the narrowing of gaps in progress that we are now seeing. While we have not yet seen an impact of our strategies on the complex issue of persistent absence, I am confident that we now at least have a means to analyse what has worked and what hasn't. This improves our chance of improving outcomes in this challenging area.

Finally, we have been encouraged in our belief that there is no need to focus largely on additional intervention which implies tacit acceptance that our 'standard' provision cannot meet the needs of disadvantaged students. We have been given confidence to focus our resources on improving the 'day to day' quality of practice as the best means to enable progress for all.

Steve Davies, Headteacher, Stocksbridge High School

9. What Does the Evidence Say?

The Sutton Trust-Education Endowment Foundation Teaching and Learning Toolkit (https://educationendowmentfoundation.org.uk/toolkit) is increasingly being used by schools as an accessible summary of educational research which provides guidance for teachers and schools on how to use their resources to improve the attainment of disadvantaged pupils. At the time of writing, the Toolkit currently covers 34 topics, each summarised in terms of their average impact on attainment, the strength of the evidence supporting them and their cost.

The EEF website says:

We know that the relationship between spending and pupil outcomes is not simple. Per pupil spending increased by 85% between 1997 and 2011, but improvements in pupil outcomes were marginal on most measures. At school level, it is clear that different ways of spending school budgets can have very different impacts on pupil attainment, and choosing what to prioritise is not easy. Even once a decision to implement a particular strategy has been taken there are a wide variety of factors which determine its impact. We believe that educational research can help schools get the maximum 'educational bang for their buck', both in terms of making an initial choice between strategies, and in implementing a strategy as effectively as possible.

One particular spending decision which research can inform is how to spend the Pupil Premium. The Toolkit ranks a range of approaches by:

- *Average impact*
- *Cost*
- *Strength of evidence*

At the last count, 65% of school leaders were now informing their decision making using the Toolkit. As Sir John Dunford and Baroness Estelle Morris have both said, the Toolkit puts us on an irreversible path towards a more evidence based profession.

An Updated Practical Guide to the Pupil Premium

The most important element of any initiative is the quality of the person delivering it. Strong relationships between teacher and learner are fundamental. Figure 7 is a graph which plots impact against cost for various interventions.

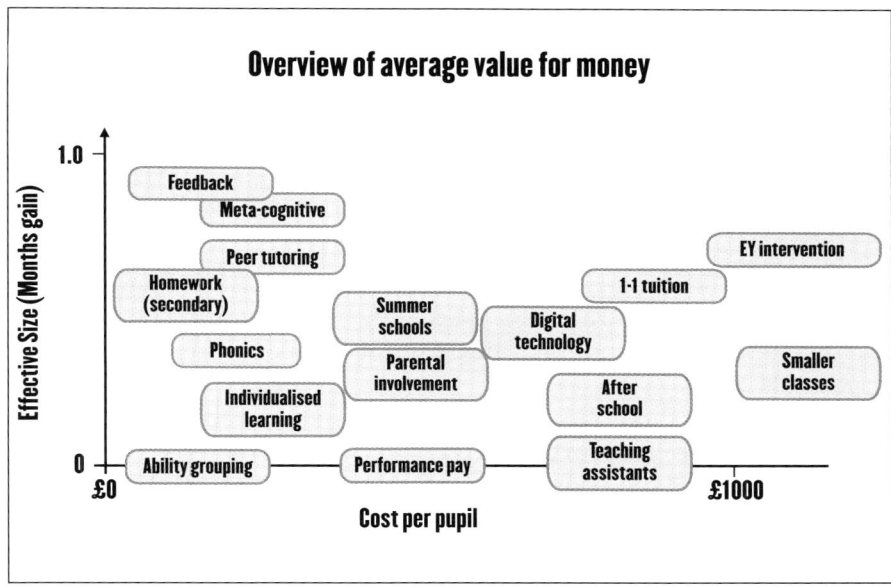

Figure 7: Overview of average value for money: Sutton Trust EEF – Teaching and Learning Toolkit

The EEF Toolkit is very useful on many levels. Equally it is important to reiterate that schools must properly engage with current research and not follow it blindly without considering the context of their own school. Schools might say they have 'done' feedback or metacognition, but it is important to interrogate evidence carefully. Be informed by it and reflect. Pause ... Research should not create unchallengeable orthodoxies or stifle innovation. An evidence-informed profession will develop from the classroom, where teachers learn from the toolkit. Teachers can ensure that their practice in its unique context is informed by evidence. A profession that effectively evaluates what it does is critically important.

10. Early Years Premium

The Early Years Pupil Premium is additional funding for Early Years settings to improve outcomes for disadvantaged three and four year-olds. Four year-olds in primary school reception classes who already receive the school-age Pupil Premium are not eligible for the Early Years Premium.

The DfE website provides more information about eligibility and registration, including signposting to the eligibility checking system and guidance for children who are (or have been) looked after by the local authority.

In 2015/16, Early Years providers receive £302.10 for each eligible child who takes up the full 570 hours of state-funded early education they are entitled to. Local Authorities are responsible for the distribution of funding. They cannot put conditions on how the funding is spent.

Early Years Pupil Premium funding should follow the eligible child rather than the provider.

The DfE website provides more information on this[8] – but it is important to note that this is a mechanism for getting funding into settings, rather than a formula for how it should be spent. As with the Pupil Premium, it is *outcomes* that matter.

Early Years providers can learn from the introduction of the Pupil Premium in schools. Good practice strategies for the Pupil Premium will apply to the Early Years Pupil Premium. Ensure that everyday practice is excellent rather than looking for golden tickets.

What does the evidence say?

The Education Endowment Foundation has produced an Early Years Toolkit[9], mirroring the Teaching and Learning Toolkit. The EEF website says:

The Early Years Toolkit is an accessible summary of educational research that provides guidance for Early Years professionals on how to use their resources to improve the learning of disadvantaged children. The Toolkit currently covers 12 topics, each summarised in terms of their average impact on learning, the strength of the evidence supporting them and their cost. Figure 8 is a synthesis of impact verses cost, plus strength of evidence.

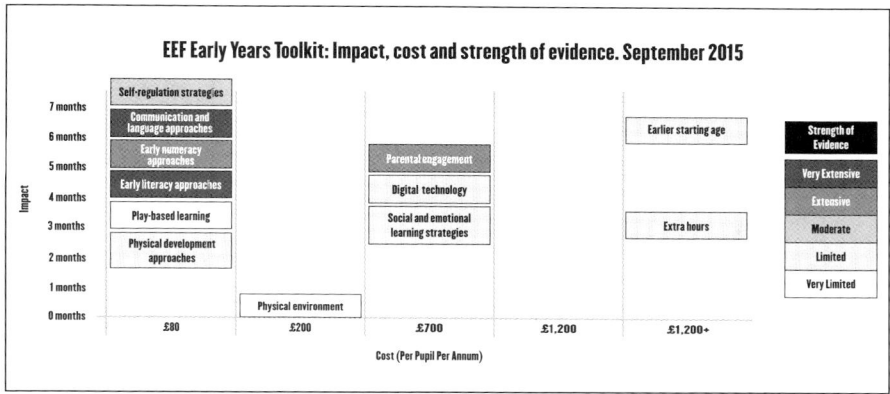

Figure 8: EEF Early Years Toolkit impact

Clearly this picture will evolve as the EEF's evidence bank evolves, but the high impact, low cost approaches all build on exisiting good practice. Interestingly, approaches that might intuitively feel right (such as extra hours) are very high cost for impact – though it should be acknowledged that evidence on this is still relatively limited. What matters is what you do with the extra time, not having the extra time in its own right.

11. Teaching Assistants

Schools which are successful with the Pupil Premium tend to fund the professional development of their Teaching Assistants with a focus on their disadvantaged learners, rather than the actual roles themselves. Encouragingly, there is a growing bank of research into the effective use of TAs. The 2015 report by the Education Endowment Foundation, makes the following seven key recommendations.[10]

It is important to work to these recommendations when planning the work of TAs.

- Teaching Assistants shouldn't be used as substitute teachers for low-attaining pupils.
- Use Teaching Assistants to add value to what teachers do, not replace them.
- Use Teaching Assistants to help pupils develop independent study skills and manage their own learning.
- Ensure Teaching Assistants are fully prepared for their role in the classroom through out of class liaison with teachers.
- Use Teaching Assistants to deliver high-quality one-to-one and small group support using structured interventions.
- Adopt evidence-based interventions to support Teaching Assistants in their small group and one-to-one instruction.
- It is important that what students learn from Teaching Assistants complements what they are being taught in the classroom.

This work has been transformational in encouraging schools to re-think their approach to narrowing gaps. It is crucial that schools interrogate evidence and interpret what it might mean for their own institution.

> **Recommended Reading**
> Webster, R., Russell, A. and Blatchford, P. (2016) *Maximising the impact of teaching assistants: Guidance for school leaders and teachers. Second edition,* Oxon: Routledge.[11]
>
> Bosanquet, P., Radford, J. and Webster, R. (2016) *The Teaching Assistant's Guide to Effective Interaction: How to maximise your practice*, Oxon: Routledge.[12]

The initial evidence of impact for Teaching Assistants was controversial. It suggests that Teaching Assistants are not the most effective way of raising attainment. However, there is a drive and passion in many Teaching Assistants to have a positive impact.

It is important to understand that, whilst the pay is low, full time Teaching Assistants are a £20,000 flexible resource which can be nurtured and grown, so we should expect an impact. We need to reflect on how to make sure that Teaching Assistants realise their potential. Teaching Assistants change lives at their best. To make this point, Charlie Henry, HMI, says that he rarely criticises Teaching Assistants, but he regularly has to criticise the management of them.

If we have professionally trained Teaching Assistants, working consistently, accessing model professional development and being well led and managed, then they will move across the arc on the EEF graph and become better value for money.

Other evidence published by the EEF supports the view that high-quality, well-trained, and expertly deployed Teaching Assistants have a positive impact.[13]

Sometimes, it is not *what* you do but *how* you do it.

The National Education Trust has put together a checklist to think about in relation to effective use of Teaching Assistants:

- Are you giving regular appraisal to the Teaching Assistants?
- Do you require minimum qualifications and/or experience?
- Do you ensure you provide reasonable and high quality CPD opportunities for support staff?
- Do you provide reasonable opportunities for joint planning?
- Do your support staff get high quality performance management?
- Do you have a system which formally requires Teaching Assistants to record their impact on pupils' progress each week?
- Have you accessed good practice resources and case studies on Teaching Assistant deployment?
- Have you audited Teaching Assistants' wider skills? (Many schools are missing out on hidden talents, especially in relation to languages, vocational skills and more.)

12. What Works For Those With Barriers in the Classroom

Good professional development is fundamental

The consistent feature of 'what works' for Pupil Premium pupils works for all pupils. Excellent teaching is crucial. Feedback and metacognition, at the top of the impact and value for money in the EEF Toolkit, are about good teaching.

Charlie Henry, HMI, Ofsted's lead for special educational needs, outlines the 'what works for some works for all' point when speaking powerfully about the ingredients of success for SEN pupils.[14] They are:

- High aspirations for the achievement of pupils.
- Good teaching and learning for all pupils.
- Provision based on careful analysis of need, close monitoring of each individual's progress and a shared perception of desired outcomes.
- Evaluation of the effectiveness of provision at all levels in helping to improve opportunities and progress.
- Leaders who look to improve general provision to meet a wider range of needs rather than always increasing additional provision.
- Swift, timely changes to provision, by individual providers and local areas, as a result of evaluating achievement and well-being.
- Clear and detailed understanding of 'next steps', based on shared perceptions of the desired outcomes.
- Focus on pupils' starting points – exceeding expected progress.

- Regularly and accurately monitored data on the progress and attainment of pupils.
- Extensively evaluated interventions.
- Evaluating a wide range of data and using it effectively to improve standards and better provision.

There is nothing surprising on this list, and of course, many SEN pupils will also be eligible for Pupil Premium. This makes adopting best practice all the more important. However, not all schools act on, or feel able to act on, the available information.

Effective feedback, teaching children metacognition, and collaborative learning are all hard to do well, and to sustain. They are about consistently excellent teaching. Spending money on increasing leadership capacity and securing high quality professional development to ensure excellence are critical.

★★★★

There is a risk that teachers and school leaders see the Pupil Premium as encouragement for the idea that you can 'buy' something that is going to fix the complex range of challenges that are associated with poverty. Schools cannot prevent poverty, but they can go some way to reducing its effect if they focus on initiatives that raise attainment by improving teaching and learning, directly or indirectly. Teaching quality counts most.

To give an example, on a visit to a school during a recent Pupil Premium review, there was a breathtakingly good teaching assistant leading a reading intervention. Seeing a little boy – starting the class with his shoulders slouched, looking down – coming to life and making visible progress in learning to read was incredibly moving. The key issue was that it was no way evident that the person leading the session was a teaching assistant. Impact counts.

This is where high quality professional development matters. Professor Robert Coe describes the kind of professional support which can best help learners.[15] It should be:

- Intense: at least 15 contact hours, preferably 50.
- Sustained: over at least two terms.
- Content focused: on teachers' knowledge of subject content and how students learn it.
- Active: opportunities to try it out and discuss.
- Supported: external feedback and networks to improve and sustain.
- Evidence-based: promotes strategies supported by robust evaluation evidence.

Effective leaders recognise the importance of well-constructed, in-house professional development, and ensure that their Pupil Premium funded activities are delivered by high quality, trained staff, with a clear understanding of the objectives of the programme. As a result, they invest in teacher and support staff training, which impacts on learning.

13. Transition

Transition from primary to secondary school is a critical time for disadvantaged learners. When resilience and focus in learning are needed most, the tectonic plates of school culture and environment shift markedly under the feet of children who are making the leap at 11+.

The failure to improve the process of transition is one of the major challenges facing our education system. It is a problem that seems often to be ignored by policy makers, and the accountability chasm encourages inertia in tackling the problem system-wide. However, there are effective actions which schools can take tomorrow:

- To encourage sharing in the use of the Pupil Premium in the long term, primary schools often keep a file with a record of interventions which disadvantaged children have taken part in, and their impact. This can be passed on to secondary schools so that they can target their resources more appropriately.

- Children should take books with them into Key Stage 3 to enable teachers to get a deeper understanding of strengths and weaknesses in primary school. Key Stage 3 practitioners should also have a good understanding of the Primary National Curriculum.

- Create a Year 7 playground to ease children into secondary school life.

- Use teachers with strong experience of the primary curriculum to provide additional and extra support in Year 7 where appropriate.

- Mentoring and advocacy can be highly effective for some learners.

- Teaching staff can play an effective role in maintaining primary-secondary relationships, but it needs to be a key part of their role, rather than an add-on.

There are many more ideas about this available in Ofsted's recent report on Key Stage 3 – more detail here: https://www.gov.uk/government/publications/key-stage-3-the-wasted-years.[16]

The important thing, from the pupil's perspective, is that schools share information so they can better understand learners. Secondary schools could provide more information about the life skills young people need to make a great start to Key Stage 3. Primary schools need to encourage independence, particularly if a student has been working closely with one teaching assistant for a long period of time. This approach, whilst well meaning, can create additional barriers.

Transition means that less resilient learners are at risk of falling further behind during what can be a daunting experience. Special schools and those schools with high numbers of service families' children are rich resources for effective approaches to transition. When systems work well, these schools prepare for the individual pupil, making sure that children arriving at their new school glide into the new learning environment, rather than land with a crash. The principle is that the destination school and class needs to be prepared for the arriving learner, as well as the child being prepared for their new school.

> *'When used well, Pupil Premium has the possibility to open up a whole new world for a child who may never have experienced what you and I may have always taken for granted.'*
>
> Vanessa Langley, Executive Headteacher, Sheffield

Clearly there are challenges to recreate such highly personalised approaches at scale, but at the same time it is important to learn from what can work. In the end it is local leadership and collaboration which are crucial.

Most importantly, we must avoid at all costs a culture of dismissing prior learning in Key Stage 2 at secondary level. At the same time, the shallow learning approach, as described in chapter three, where children are pulled up through repeated SATs practice to meet accountability targets in Year 6, only serves to enhance the view of some Key Stage 3 teachers that many children cannot successfully access the secondary curriculum. A better grasp of a learner's strengths and weaknesses can help negate these views, as can a better understanding of progress up to and during transition.

Barriers to learning that are common in disadvantaged pupils, with a change of schools, and curriculum, exacerbate the challenges for less resilient learners.

Teaching metacognition may well be the key. Research at Rosendale Primary School[17] in Lambeth indicates that metacognition can help create successful learners who have:

- Clear understanding of what they do and do not know.
- Ability to plan an approach to problems.
- Ability to seek out information.
- Ability to check on their progress.
- Ability to change strategies when things go wrong.

These characteristics may sustain learners during the period of transition. By teaching children metacognition in Year 6, with those themes picked up again in Year 7 to ensure a continuum, learners can go back to what has helped them previously to overcome future challenges.

Whatever actions schools take, the fog of accountability targets and responsibility for outcomes should not deter schools from ensuring that all learners have solid foundations, and that the building blocks are secure to enable learning continuity during one of the most vulnerable times in their schooling.

> *'In our schools, we expect our disadvantaged pupils to leave EYFS 'school ready', to leave primary 'secondary ready', and when they leave school all young people should be 'life ready'.*
>
> Rebecca Clark, National Director, Oasis Community Learning

14. Governance

Governors have a crucial role to play in ensuring that Pupil Premium activity has the maximum impact and value for money. Informed discussions with governors from good schools demonstrate an understanding of activity and impact of the Pupil Premium in their school. Governors and leaders also need to have discussions about what to stop doing because it is not working so well.

Nationally, governance is patchy with the Pupil Premium, but a leading example is a Special School we have worked with in the Midlands. Governors there have a detailed knowledge of the range of activities undertaken with Pupil Premium funding, as well as an understanding of the aims and actual impact.

There is a clear channel for regular updates on activity and impact. Governors receive details of pupils (anonymised) in receipt of Pupil Premium funding. They are informed about what individual pupil requirements are, what intervention each pupil receives, what impact is expected and a summary evaluation for each pupil.

> *'A personalised curriculum is fundamental to meeting the individual learning needs of our pupils. Pupil Premium is key in helping us to achieve this.'*
>
> Derek Fance, Primary School Headteacher, Warwickshire

Information is also provided at a higher level, with governors informed about the effect of particular interventions on groups of pupils, as well as the overall impact of a range of interventions on an individual pupil. This allows governors to act as 'critical friends' to the school, and ensure that the Pupil Premium is being spent in a way that has most benefit; it enables a professional discourse.

Our work nationally on governance shows that challenge and support are of varying quality. There are some excellent examples of good practice, but also a significant minority of governors who have very limited knowledge of the attainment gap in their school, how much money is received, how it is being spent and what the impact of funding is.

In effective governing bodies, the three keys are:

- Training is given for governors on evaluating the impact of interventions on attitudes, learning behaviours, well being, aspirations and other outcomes as well as on academic measures.
- Governing bodies nominate an interested and committed Pupil Premium governor to work with the school leadership team to ensure there is secure knowledge across all governors of Pupil Premium funded activity and impact.
- Most governors can answer the questions in the Analysis and Challenge for Schools (see page 127).

More help is at hand from the National Governors Association. They have provided a detailed set of questions that should enable effective challenge and support.

Questions for Governing Bodies to Ask: Pupil Premium

Are we making best use of the Pupil Premium?

For Governing Bodies:

- Can we identify how much money is allocated to the school for the Pupil Premium?
  - Is it identified in the school's budget planning?
  - Can we identify the Pupil Premium funding separately to any other funding for disadvantaged pupils?
- In determining the strategy for spending the Pupil Premium have we considered the Ofsted/Education Endowment Foundation information about what methods are effective in raising attainment for disadvantaged pupils?
- Do the school's improvement/action plans identify whether there are any issues in the performance of pupils who are eligible for the Pupil Premium?
- Do the actions noted for improving outcomes for Pupil Premium pupils:
  - give details of how the resources are to be allocated?
  - give an overview of the actions to be taken?
  - give a summary of the expected outcomes?
  - identify ways of monitoring the effectiveness of these actions as they are ongoing and note who will be responsible for ensuring that this information is passed to governors?
  - explain what will be evaluated at the end of the action and what measures of success will be applied?
- Will we know and be able to intervene quickly to request remedial action if outcomes are not improving in the way that we want them to?

For Senior Leaders

- Have you checked the KeytoSuccess website to ensure that you have a full list of all eligible pupils – given that some of the children will not currently be claiming FSM.
- Are staff aware of which pupils are Pupil Premium children

and the possible support and expected intervention? Have all staff received the training they need to effectively support disadvantaged children?
- Is the school using its best staff (teachers and support staff) with Pupil Premium children?
- What processes have you put in place to evaluate whether the intervention strategies are working?
- Are the progress and outcomes of eligible pupils identified and analysed by the school's tracking systems? How will you report this information to governors in a way that enables them to see clearly whether the gap in the performance of eligible pupils and other pupils is closing?
- On the school website, how good is the account of Pupil Premium spending? In particular, does it describe the impact of Pupil Premium strategies?
- Do the school's systems enable you to give a clear picture to governors about the progress and attainment of pupils who are eligible for the Pupil Premium in all year groups across the school, not just those at the end of Key Stages?
- Are there gaps in the attainment of pupils who are eligible for the Pupil Premium and those who are not and, if so, are eligible pupils making accelerated progress – to allow the gaps to close?
- Are you tracking the attendance, punctuality and behaviour (particularly exclusions) of this group and taking action to address any differences?
- Have you looked at the websites of other similar schools to see what interventions they are using?
- How do you promote awareness of FSM eligibility to encourage all eligible pupils to claim?

Courtesy, the National Governors Association.[18]

15. Active Ingredients – Case Studies

1. **Lillington Primary School (Warwickshire)** invested heavily in 'Outstanding Teacher Training Intervention' for five of its teachers as part of its wider strategy to improve pupil outcomes. The school measured impact carefully, spent time discussing strengths, weaknesses and areas for improvement (rather than getting bogged down in giving Ofsted-style grades), and ensured intervention was evidence-based and only delivered with excellence. Enrichment and pastoral activities run alongside teaching improvements. All pupils have a learning mentor so that every child is stretched as an individual, regardless of their starting point.

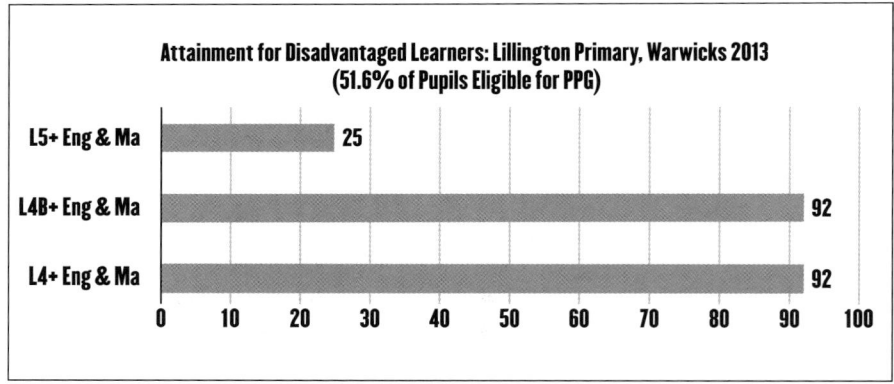

Figure 9: Attainment for disadvantaged learners at Lillington Primary School, Warwickshire

This school not only saw a dramatic improvement in its quality of teaching and SATs results, as well as a narrowing of the gap; it also saw a dramatic drop in teacher absence and its work with the Pupil Premium has been highly commended nationally.

The Head of Lillington Primary school recognised the need to focus on the team he worked with, to improve the teaching quality so that disadvantaged learners could catch up. He also recognised that there are no quick fixes. This has been transformational for learners.[19]

★★★★

> '*The Pupil Premium has helped to turn the spotlight on the most vulnerable children in our country. It has challenged us not to think of short term alternatives to support these learners, but to fundamentally change their day-to-day experience of schools.*'
>
> Steve Davies, Secondary School Headteacher, Sheffield

2. **Raynham Primary (Enfield)** was struggling to improve their pupils' attainment levels. They tried intervention through Teaching Assistants and through graduates, but they were unsuccessful. There was limited impact despite extensive training. So they introduced a programme where retired, experienced teachers in their 70s, who no longer wanted to work full time, led the interventions. The scheme has been enormously successful.

These experienced teachers capitalise on their years in the classroom. Using detailed data analysis of individual children, they work with small groups to address 'shared gaps', assess pupil understanding and address needs so that pupils can quickly return to the classroom.

One of the aspects that stands out in much of the debate about improving outcomes for learners is a lack of reference to the curriculum. To promote deep rather than shallow learning, schools like Raynham link changes to the curriculum with their plans for the Pupil Premium. Schools which are successful in raising attainment for disadvantaged children have committed teachers, a whole community ambition, a culturally relevant curriculum, and a vision for pupils which runs through the school as consistent as Brighton through a stick of rock.[20]

★★★★

3. **Downs School (Harlow)**,[21] the newly appointed Headteacher sought to use the Pupil Premium to strengthen the leadership of outcomes for disadvantaged pupils. A significant proportion of the funding has been spent on securing a leadership role with a main focus on driving better outcomes for disadvantaged pupils across the school. The role was not to be responsible for every pupil, but to ensure that high quality interventions and excellent teaching are standard. The leadership role also ensures effective quality monitoring and impact evaluation are sacrosanct. In 2015, outcomes for disadvantaged learners have improved from 40% L4+ RWM combined to over 80%.

4. **Bishop Challoner Catholic Girls' School (Tower Hamlets)** has demonstrated rapid success in supporting the progress and attainment of disadvantaged pupils.

As a school in a Local Authority identified as having the highest levels of child poverty in the UK, many students experience in some way the known effects of poverty and deprivation: low levels of aspiration and expectations; poor literacy and numeracy; lack of cultural enrichment; lack of family experience of university and professional careers; broken family structures; poor diet.

With over 50% of the school identified as disadvantaged under the Pupil Premium indicator, the senior leadership team made the acute analytical decision that funding should be used to impact on whole school improvement and transformation across the local federation.

The principle vision is that improving the quality of teaching and learning in all lessons and expanding the capacity of the federation means that all pupils benefit. The vision includes individualised, specific and methodical support over a period of time which has a clear focus on English, Maths and Science. The school has reaped the rewards, particularly in relation to the increasing proportion of disadvantaged learners achieving grades B, A and A*.

Beyond the focus on those academic outcomes, the school has also worked to ensure that the drive to tackle educational disadvantage comes from the middle. Year group leaders were asked to focus on a group of ten disadvantaged learners each week over a term and have a tactful conversation with them about their lives in general – school life, home life, wellbeing, whether home is suitable for study. In some cases they used data to feed back on progress and punctuality/attendance to date.

This feedback was collated and enabled senior and middle leaders to have an informed planning session about how to support their young people from an evidence base.

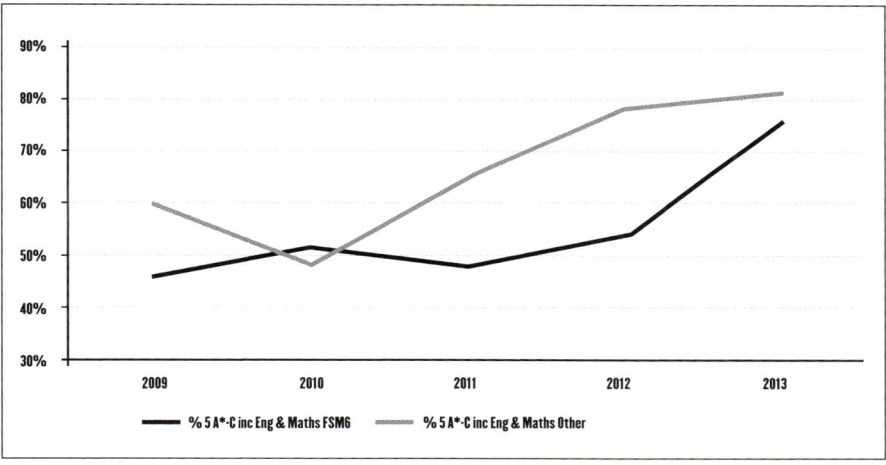

Figure 10: Attainment gap at Bishop Challoner Girls' School 2009-2013

★★★★

5. **Oakdene Primary (Stockton-on-Tees)** is an excellent school in exceptionally challenging circumstances which declares that the sparkling curriculum, moulded and shaped to generate interest and intrigue in their pupils, their families and their teachers, is key to its success. This is backed up with the Pupil Premium being used to train and develop teachers and support staff to have the tools, expertise and knowledge to teach that curriculum so that children,

often living difficult lives, are leaving with high attainment and a deep love of learning.

The rich community-relevant curriculum – a great mix of romance and rigour – means that the funding is used, indeed is targeted, to meet the needs of every learner in a school community with over 50% of learners from disadvantaged backgrounds, many of whom have special educational needs.[22]

> ### A Need for Knowledge of the World Around Us...
> - 1 in 4 does not know a chick is a baby chicken
> - 1 in 5 doesn't know pork comes from pigs
> - 29% of 5-8 year olds think cheese comes from plants
> - 34% think pasta comes from animals
> - 18% think fish fingers come from chicken
>
> *Survey of 1,000 UK children aged 5-11 carried out in May 2015 on behalf of LEAF, Linking Environment and Farming. British Nutrition Foundation national pupil survey of 27,500 children, 2013.*[23]

★★★★

6. **St Joseph's Catholic Primary (Camden)** provides one of the most interesting examples on how to use the Pupil Premium. Its achievement statistics speak for themselves. (See Figure 11.)

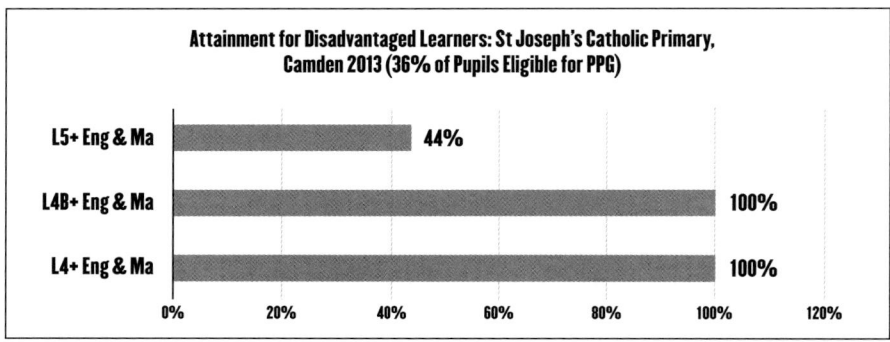

Figure 11: Attainment for disadvantaged learners at St Joseph's Catholic Primary School, Camden

The inner urban school takes the view that – to offer children exceptional life chances – at the end of Key Stage 1, every child, regardless of background, should attain a Level 2b+. At the end of Key Stage 2, 100% of pupils should be at Level 4a+, 70% of pupils at a secure Level 5+ and 30% of children at Level 6 in Maths.

The school's mantra is ambition, creativity and expertise, saying it is the responsibility of the school to enable the child to make progress, clearly demonstrating that equal opportunity is not the same as equal provision.

Spending money on	Impact/Benefit /Enables
Increase capacity of SLT: *The Leadership taking responsibility*	To run and monitor interventions across the school To ensure T&L are good or outstanding To provide effective training for ALL staff To work with outside agencies and vulnerable children
EY Intervention	To identify vulnerable children who need additional support and plan provision To provide parent workshops in literacy and maths
Extracurricular trips and activities	To enhance the curriculum, ensure children are able to participate, and to give children the opportunity to experience new and challenging activities
High quality and focused training for all staff – including specialist subject knowledge	To ensure that children have personalised support to meet their needs So highly trained TAs run evidence based interventions To develop and grow a specialist maths teacher
Increase capacity to run catch up programmes	To accelerate progress in maths and literacy in KS2 to ensure children are working at or above age related expectations
Funding club activities	To ensure the children are able to participate and to give children the opportunity to experience new and challenging activities outside of school
Achievement for All	Achievement for All is a whole-school approach to school improvement, which has had demonstrable success in improving rates of progress for vulnerable pupils.

Table 3: Pupil Premium Statement: St Joseph's Catholic Primary School, Camden 2013/14

Put simply, the school leadership takes ownership. They create the time, space and capacity to ensure excellence as standard in everything they do.[24]

16. Special Schools

Special Schools need to evaluate the degree to which socio-economic background is impacting on outcomes. In doing this, they need to consider to what extent the socio-economic background is either a greater limiting factor than the learning disability, or the extent to which it provides a different challenge from that posed by the learning disability.

In Special School provision there are interesting questions about how the additional funding can be utilised in such a way that it will have a meaningful impact on pupil outcomes. This is because the primary barrier to learning is usually developmental rather than socio-economic.

When planning for the use of the Pupil Premium, Frank Wise Special School in Oxfordshire looked beyond the notion of successful outcomes being based on knowledge and skills and also considered the application of what has already been learned within functional contexts.

This enabled the school to identify where socio-economic background may begin to influence more, particularly around the further development of socially appropriate behaviours and socially based communication.

The difficulty is that access to effectively staffed, developmentally and age-appropriate social opportunities can be limited, expensive and logistically challenging. Yet without access to such experiences there is a risk that children may not be able to apply the social and communication skills being developed at school.

To overcome this challenge in a sustainable way, the school used Pupil Premium funding to contribute to the employment of an Out of School Liaison Officer (OSLO) to secure further funding for access and act as a broker between providers of social opportunity and families who may want to take up those opportunities but have practical barriers to overcome.

The OSLO is an integral position in the school, supporting the school's aim and ethos. This helps to promote the school's philosophy within the local area, developing a community-wide belief in the potential of school pupils, recognising they have both the right and ability to be active contributors to the community in which they live.[25]

> *'We have high expectations for all of our pupils and the Pupil Premium Grant has supported us in providing personalised learning programmes to raise attainment and enrich the experiences of our more vulnerable pupils.'*
>
> Rosie Alexander, Primary Headteacher, Hertfordshire

The Pupil Premium Plus is potentially a great boost for special schools, for many will get an increase in funding as pupils with SEN are disproportionately 'looked after'.

> **TALBOT Specialist School in Sheffield** *has carried out some very interesting Action Research into how physical exercise can support students that have complex learning difficulties to better engage with their learning.*[7]

Limpsfield Grange School is a special school in Surrey for girls between the ages of 11-16. The school also offers residential provision, which is accessed by the majority of students attending Limpsfield Grange across a school week. It caters for students with a wide range of needs including Autism and Asperger's; students who have communication and interaction difficulties; and students who due to their physical or emotional vulnerabilities would not have the resilience to succeed in a mainstream setting.

The spending offers a really interesting example of a school that has focused on ensuring that individual students in receipt of the Pupil Premium meet their bespoke targets. In particular the school has concentrated on developing literacy and numeracy skills for Pupil Premium learners in order to increase access to the rest of the curriculum. The school uses a number of interventions to support improving literacy and numeracy skills including:

- GCSE Statistics for more able learners
- Up-levelling writing groups
- Spelling City
- Mathletics for KS3 students
- Comprehension sessions
- Reading for meaning and developing inference skill sessions
- GCSE booster sessions for English

Many students have difficulties with their communication and interaction skills associated with their autism, mental health needs or due to the high levels of social anxiety that they experience. The majority of students at Limpsfield Grange also require high levels of support to help them to understand their own thoughts and feelings, and how these impact on other people. To support these needs, the school has used some of its funding for a Family Partnership Practitioner who has been working with identified students and their families to help promote communication and interaction skills, with the aim of enabling students to be able to identify and label their emotions. This improves the students' ability to be ready to learn, and enables them to access learning. This work has included:

- 'Drawing and talking' therapy sessions for small groups of identified students to develop self-awareness and identify strategies to help promote positive communication and interaction skills.
- One-to-one support with students with fixed and inflexible thinking to develop strategies for communicating with their peers.
- Running focus groups in the residential setting which work with identified students on their statemented needs.
- 'Sand Play' therapy sessions for students who have difficulty labelling and identifying their emotions.
- Supporting students to access a self-esteem and body image course.
- How to stay safe on the internet sessions with students at risk of online sexual exploitation.

The school expects that these interventions will enable the identified students to improve their communication skills, their access to the curriculum and their engagement and attitude to learning. The senior leadership team monitor the pupil spend per pupil each week, and monitor outcomes and impact regularly to ensure that Pupil Premium money spent is directly linked to improved student outcomes. Interestingly, the school invites parents to speak with the leadership team if they have any concerns about how the funding is being used, linking back to the original mission to focus on the individual.

Seamus Oates, Executive Headteacher of TBAP Trust, London, says that it is difficult to talk about the use of Pupil Premium in isolation. Within the Trust it is used as part of a whole school model and approach. The TBAP Trust consists of seven Alternative Provision Academies, several of which used to be Pupil Referral Units (PRUs) and also a commissioning and school support team. At TBAP, they ensure that every student has a personalised offer of learning, and they achieve this through excellent knowledge of their students. Before any student arrives at a TBAP school, they have a week long assessment centre, where they will undergo various assessments to help give the staff at the schools an idea of each student's abilities and needs. Once they are in school, they are assessed regularly allowing staff to understand each pupil's progress and adjust the programme or their teaching accordingly.[26]

17. Looked After Children (LAC)

Children in care and children who have been adopted or who are on special guardianship orders or residence orders receive the Pupil Premium Plus, which is £1,900 per annum. This funding is paid to schools for adopted and SGO/RO children, but the funding for children in care now goes to local authorities for the head of the Virtual School to manage. This postholder – a statutory requirement for local authorities under the Children and Families Act 2014 – carries out the duty of local authorities to promote the education of children in care.

Children in care are amongst the lowest performing groups of any children. In 2014, only 12% attained five or more GCSEs at A*-C including English and mathematics, and only around 30% made three or more levels of progress from Key Stage 2 in English or mathematics. Only 58% of 19 year-old care leavers were in education, employment or training in March 2013.

The gaps at Key Stages 1 and 2, though narrower, are still concerning. Children in care are ten times more likely to have a statement of SEN than their peers (severe SEN can mean that parents and carers struggle to cope), and are more likely to be excluded. Frequent changes of carers and schools usually compound the problem. There is less evidence about the attainment of adopted/SGO/RO children but the message is clear – children who have endured early abuse and neglect can hugely underachieve in education, even if they have lived in caring and supportive homes for many years.

So, what works? All of the strategies written about in other chapters in this book are just as applicable to children in care. Small group tuition, though expensive, is regarded by many to be one of the most effective strategies since a good tutor will identify the gaps in learning and teach accordingly.

Evidence to support this comes from several sources including the Department for Education and research by Robert Flynn[27] in Canada. The Department for Education also identifies the following as crucial to educational success:

- Placement stability – of home and school.
- Length of time in care – the longer a child is in one care placement the better they are likely to achieve.
- Attending a school that meets the child's assessed needs, ie high academic expectations.

Furthermore, better training in attachment and trauma may help. Many children looked after need people around them who understand how attachment trauma and loss can rewire neurological pathways to be a significant barrier to learning.

Often the missing ingredient is a shared professional understanding and language between schools, social workers and carers of the effects of trauma on a child's capacity to succeed within school. Attachment and trauma have long been a part of social care and carer training but for some reason it has largely bypassed teacher training and school-based professional development.[28]

Recent neuro-scientific research now underpins earlier psychological research and shows how the affected child's brain simply isn't wired to cope with schooling. If you've grown up in fear, unable to control your anger or impulses and believe you are worthless then schools, however welcoming, seem like hostile battlegrounds; lessons – intriguing and challenging to most – can trigger overwhelming stress.

Looked After Children: Some Data (2014)

- 68% of looked-after children achieved Level 4 in reading, compared with 89% of others.
- The gap at 11 is even larger in writing and mathematics.
- 12% of looked-after children achieved 5+ GCSEs at A*-CEM, compared with 53% of others.
- 33% of care leavers become NEET, compared with 13% of all young people.
- 6% of care leavers go to university, compared with 40% of others.
- This is less than the percentage of care leavers who go to prison.
- 67% of looked-after children have SEN compared with 18% of the total population. Of those, 29% have a statement compared with 2.8% of all children.
- 62% of children become looked-after as a result of abuse or neglect and they have a much higher incidence of mental health problems.

Data courtesy of Sir John Dunford.[29]

We still have distance to travel before arriving at a school system better attuned to help these most vulnerable children cope, but work by writers like Louise Bomber[30] point the way. What is also needed is hard edged research to show what works for the children when nothing else in the teacher's toolkit seems to.

Adoption is For Life

Best practice ensures that Personal Education Plans continue once children have been formally adopted or placed in long term foster care. The spending of Pupil Premium funding should be agreed by the school, pupil and parent/carer voice.

Many placements are successful for the first 12 months, but after this period the family unit can be vulnerable. The support appears to stop. We need to recognise that there is a need for schools to be proactive, for example, working with post-adoption support groups and formalising regular Team Around Family meetings.

All school staff (not just teachers) should attend training for the attachment-friendly school, and all staff should agree the terminology to use e.g 'birthparent' rather than 'real' mum or dad.

Teachers should be encouraged to map out their curriculum and identify areas which may be sensitive. For example, 'bring in a photograph of when you were a baby'. At the same time, staff need to ensure that a balance of sensitivity is achieved without going to extremes. I learned with horror about an adopted child who was excluded from a task involving writing to a pen pal about family life for fear of upsetting. Sensitivity and understanding are what is required.

With permission, we have organised an adoption/long-term foster group. We meet termly, I chair it as the LAC champion – every school should have one to build understanding of this vulnerable group. It was set up to make the pupils aware that they are special and unique but not alone. There are 25 children in the group currently. It is in its infancy but so far it has been incredibly powerful. At the first meeting I shared a presentation of well-known characters, asking in turn what did we know about each person, e.g. Steve Jobs, Harry Potter. The common thread was that all had been adopted and they could see how successful they had been.

Liz Bramley, Headteacher and Adoption Champion

18. Successful Schools and the Pupil Premium

In his remarkable book *The Diving Bell and the Butterfly*, Jean Dominique Bauby narrates his story by blinking one eyelid whilst experiencing 'locked-in syndrome'. The metaphor is that his body is weighed down by the diving bell of disability, whilst his mind is still free to 'write' – what has been described by *The Financial Times* as 'one of the great books of the century.'[31]

Bauby offers two thoughts which one might relate to disadvantaged learners. First, the Pupil Premium cannot entirely negate the effects of poverty on learner outcomes, but it is part of the package which schools can use to set children and young people free from the diving bell of the circumstances into which they are born. Second, it is a reminder that limits should not be set on what learners can achieve, in spite of or because of their circumstances.

Schools which are successful with raising expectations and outcomes for Pupil Premium children share key common characteristics:

- Successful schools build teams where their vision is understood and pursued by the entire school community with relentless energy. At Ray Lodge Primary in Redbridge, governors, midday supervisors, pupils and teachers are all able to clearly articulate the school's values about high expectations for disadvantaged pupils. Rosendale Primary School in Lambeth bases its whole school development plan around its stated vales. When Stocksbridge High School wanted to move away from a culture of 'intervention', the Headteacher Steve Davies started by agreeing a collective mission that set out an expectation of excellent outcomes regardless of socio-economic background.

Visit Slough and Eton CE Business & Enterprise College, St Mary's CE Primary in Handsworth, The Wroxham School in Hertfordshire, Frank Wise Special School in Banbury, St Eugene De Mazenod Catholic Primary in Camden, or Oakdene Primary in Stockton and ask any member of teaching staff about the school's vision. The vision runs consistently through the school, imprinted in its DNA. Aspirations are values driven.

- Understanding attitudes to learning and family engagement, on a pupil-by-pupil basis, is vital for the successful impact of Pupil Premium spending. This is a big challenge, and one identified as 'the next step' for many school leaders, however successful they have been.

- Quality of teaching and learning counts most. Schools that create the best outcomes for pupils, recruit, train and retain great teachers and support staff. They adhere to model practice in the use of professional development. If the teaching is not consistently very good at your school, then that should be the focus for Pupil Premium funded activity – any other initiative is sticking plaster.

- They set out very clear expectations for their Pupil Premium funded activity, and monitor and evaluate rigorously to hold themselves to account.

One of the consistent features of excellent leaders is that they understand their communities to the point that they know what it is like to live their lives. As Harper Lee writes in *To Kill a Mockingbird*:[32]

"You never really understand a person until you consider things from his point of view – until you climb into his skin and walk around in it."

It is in these schools that we see national and local trends robustly challenged, with disadvantaged pupils performing at the levels their peers do nationally. These primary, special and secondary schools:

- Are open to sharing what they do, at the same time constantly looking outwards, to learn from others and to 'magpie' ideas.
- Work together to make transition almost seamless.
- Plan for the long term, asking: 'what will work in our school context, excite pupils and their families about learning'? It's not just the Pupil Premium that will help narrow the gaps.
- Have high expectations and take risks to reach their goals – they don't let accountability targets drive practice. As Phillip Pullman writes in his memorable children's horror story *Clockwork*.[33] "You don't win ... by wishing. You have to train hard, strive your upmost and sometimes that isn't enough. You have to be willing to risk failure."
- Use data to inform their practice and interventions, but don't let it become their Sargasso Sea – not everything can be measured in the same way and it is important not to get bogged down. Learning how to evaluate effectively is crucial.
- Recognise that good practice for Pupil Premium is good practice for all. It is one part of a complex jigsaw that improves outcomes. Leadership matters.

Key Ingredients

Ingredients (but not a recipe!) for success:

Leadership of the Pupil Premium is strong. It is difficult to imagine any school doing well for disadvantaged learners where the leadership is not strong, with a clear vision for disadvantaged pupils. A quick look at the leadership section in the Ofsted reports of the 2014 Pupil Premium awards illustrates this beautifully.

An Updated Practical Guide to the Pupil Premium

19. Leadership Traits

Pupil Premium Awards – Winners 2014

School Name	Ofsted Comments
Park Junior School, Shirebrook, East Midlands	Inspirational leadership from the executive headteacher and head of school has driven the excellent improvements in all areas of the school since the last inspection.
St Joseph's Catholic Primary School, Holborn, London	'Rigorous, relentless and robust' is the mantra of the headteacher and that is exactly what you find in leadership at all levels, at St Joseph's Catholic Primary School. The headteacher is passionate about personalising the learning for each unique child at the school. Consequently, this is a highly inclusive school, in which all pupils are treated equally and make outstanding progress. The exceptional headteacher has built a leadership team with an excellent range of skills, which they use to admirable effect, to drive improvements. Leaders articulate a vision for the school.
Queen's Park Academy, Bedford, East of England	Leadership and management are good. The strong and effective leadership of the headteacher, senior leaders and governing body, make a substantial impact on the academy's development, based on accurate self-evaluation.
St Francis CE (Aided) Junior School, Newton Aycliffe, North East	Senior leaders have a strong focus on raising achievement. They monitor the management of performance effectively.
All Saints CE Primary School, Whitefield, North West	Children make outstanding progress in the Early Years Foundation Stage because teaching and the leadership and management of the department are of the highest quality. Leaders and managers have an exceptionally sharp focus on how successful the school can be. They know exactly how well the school is doing and where it could do even better.
IQRA Slough Islamic Primary School, Slough, South East	A dynamic senior leadership team is now in place and together they have successfully raised standards, addressed the inadequacies in teaching and transformed pupils' behaviour.
Morice Town Primary School, Plymouth, South West	The key strength of the school's leadership and management is the way in which all members of staff and governors are enabled to operate as an effective team. Effective leadership by the headteacher, supported by other teachers and assistants, has ensured that the school continues to improve standards.
Flax Hill Junior Academy, Tamworth, West Midlands	The headteacher provides strong leadership and has high expectations for what every pupil and teacher can achieve. Governors are well informed about strengths and priorities for development and provide very good challenge and support to the headteacher and his senior leadership team.
St Andrews CE Primary School (VA), Hull, Yorkshire and the Humber	Strong drive and ambition has improved the overall effectiveness of the school in the short time since the last inspection.
Millfield Science & Performing Arts College, Thornton-Cleveleys, North West	The inspirational leadership of the Headteacher has been pivotal, but care has been taken to develop leadership and secure a strong capacity to improve further at all levels.

Table 4: Extracts on leadership for 2014 Pupil Premium award winners – Ofsted reports[34]

Leaders set the agenda and vision and follow that vision relentlessly. Leadership ensures that disadvantaged pupils have a high profile across their school. A light is shone on them. They are expected to attain well and play an important role in school life. In these schools tackling educational disadvantage is a key element of the school development plan.

Where other professionals are involved in supporting learners, leaders ensure decision making is joined up with the needs of the pupil. Teachers, leaders and intervention leads agree appropriate action, focused on gaps in learning and not national curriculum levels. Additional support is exactly that – additional and extra to the teaching in the classroom.

Funding is spent evenly throughout each year group. Schools which intervene and support early, as gaps become evident, are far less likely to be 'cohort vulnerable'.

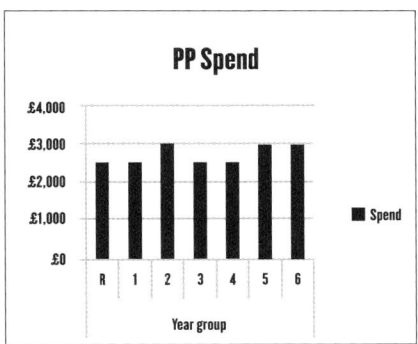
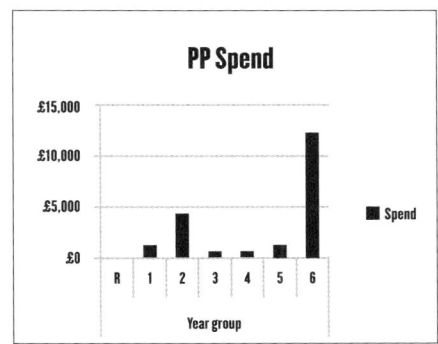

Figure 12: Pupil Premium expenditure across year groups

One of the keys to success with the leadership of the Pupil Premium is getting it out of Headteachers' offices and into classrooms. Challenging educational disadvantage should be a key driver for Middle Leaders. And teachers in the classroom should feel accountable for the outcomes of their disadvantaged pupils.

When leadership is poor, the most vulnerable are disproportionately affected.

Every adult in the school, from reception to the Headteacher's office is a leader as far as children are concerned.

> **A Lesson in Disastrous Leadership!**
> *The Raft of the Medusa*[35] – a major work in French 19th-century painting. Géricault drew his inspiration from the account of two survivors of the Medusa – a French Royal Navy frigate that set sail in 1816 to colonize Senegal. It was captained by an officer of the Ancien Régime who had not sailed for over 20 years and who ran the ship aground on a sandbank. Due to the shortage of lifeboats, those who were left behind had to build a raft for 150 souls – a construction that drifted away on a bloody 13-day odyssey that was to save only ten lives. The disaster of the shipwreck was made worse by the brutality and cannibalism that ensued.

Schools that struggle with the gap are those that are very intervention heavy, with expenditure and activity focused on pulling up children at the last minute to meet accountability targets. *Fill in cracks as they emerge rather than paper over crevasses in Year 6 – 11.* This happens when teachers have high expectations and there is an open culture when things are not working.

Narrowing the gap is not about task completion or buying something off the shelf. It's about digging deep. Building strong foundations.

High Expectations

This is the really important element of excellent leadership for disadvantaged pupils. But what does it actually mean? To me, it's the eradication of any suggestion that 'you'll never do it with these kids' or even 'you should see where they come from' (as one Chair of Governors once said to me).

High expectations are about:
- Treating every learner as an individual. Knowing their back story to understand them, not to use as an excuse.
- Not using targets that put limits on learners. We need to be wary of the tyranny of focusing on the C/D borderline when a pupil could have achieved more.
- Seeing individuals with multiple barriers as superhuman. Higher expectations mean 'labels' don't stop people doing amazing things.
- The relentless pursuit of excellence. High expectations are where the Year 3 teacher is celebrated over the Key Stage 2 results as much as the Year 6 teacher.

Identifying the Barriers and Tailoring Activities

Disadvantaged pupils are not a homogenous group. There is no such thing as a 'Pupil Premium child'. Further, the schools that serve them have different contexts. Whilst there will be similarities, disadvantaged pupils in rural Cumbria face some different challenges to those in Camden. Attendance for disadvantaged pupils in rural deprived communities can be a challenge, particularly where transport is poor.

Barriers can be varied and multiple in some cases. Children may be disadvantaged and have SEND. They may have barriers that don't come with a label such as a difficult home life, overcrowding, or difficulty in making friendships. The barriers may be the school community having low expectations of them, or, it may be inconsistent teaching and learning.

To better understand the barriers their pupils faced, Baylis Court School in Slough, a 2015 Pupil Premium award winner, interviews every student to better understand their ambitions and challenges as individuals. Don't assume your disadvantaged pupils need to do orienteering because it is what you enjoyed at that age. Find out what's missing for your pupils in your community – as a group, and as individuals.

Without that sharp look at what the challenges are in your community, schools will be throwing darts blindly. It is no good spending the Pupil Premium on improving feedback if pupils are not attending!

- If you have ability grouping in your school, review which groups your disadvantaged pupils are represented in and why.
- Monitor how much time a randomly selected group of disadvantaged pupils are spending out of the classroom over a week.

Dr Martina Lecky at Ruislip High School speaks powerfully about the need to ensure every pupil, regardless of background, has an advocate that supports them – to help them find work experience, to help them with presentation skills, to help them with university visits.

Without the support of an adult that has been there, disadvantaged pupils may just feel like they don't belong and turn away from opportunity. The Pupil Premium can ensure this is not the case.

The Pupil Premium should never just be about low attainment, it should be about tackling potential underachievement, pupil by pupil.

Getting it Right in the Classroom
What matters most is what happens in the classroom. Teachers own the success of all their learners. They don't feel that the SENCO/TA/Intervention lead is responsible. Intervention is not a first resort.

Lyon's Hall School in Essex have set aside an additional 45 minutes for their teachers to undertake research, provide one-to-one sessions, provide additional feedback sessions, plan for the needs of their disadvantaged pupils or other activities focused on improving outcomes.

The easiest way to illustrate the importance of teaching on disadvantaged pupils is with regards to feedback and marking. If you come from a very disadvantaged background, it may well be that the only feedback on your learning will come from your teachers. Quality matters.

Where intervention is required, it is important to ensure that it is additional and extra to high quality teaching in the classroom. Systems should be robust and, where possible, the interventions should be evidence based. It is well worth considering the following:

- Do teachers contribute to discussions about intervention? Are they focused on gaps in learning (or barriers to learning)? Are they involved in the commissioning of intervention? Do teachers get to observe intervention leads?

- Does the intervention focus on
  a) quality
  b) specific success criteria
  c) time limited
  d) linked to learning in the classroom?

- Where interventions are focused on nurture, is there a clear expectation about getting children learning as soon as possible?

- Is monitoring of quality and evaluation of outcome frequent and robust?

School culture is really important too. Children and young people learn a great deal from their mistakes. One of the challenges some of our disadvantaged pupils face is a fear of failure, sometimes meaning they'll avoid challenge all together. We cannot expect young people to learn and understand the purpose of failure if teachers themselves are scared to experiment and get it wrong sometimes too.

Growth Mindset

'If we accept the fact that highly effective teaching can add value to the performance of all children but especially to disadvantaged children, then I would argue that it is essential that schools 'get it right' in the classroom. This becomes even more challenging when we review how long we have spent trying to 'get it right' and the small impact that we have had so far on closing the achievement gap.

I take heart, however, from the growing body of evidence based practice being created by schools and other organisations. This body of evidence can help us to select proven approaches and strategies, that research shows can make a marked difference to outcomes for disadvantaged children. More than this though, we need to be challenging long established classroom practices that research has shown have a negative impact on disadvantaged children.

Setting, streaming or grouping children by ability has a proven negative impact on disadvantaged children, yet you will still see it happening in schools up and down the country. Where is the evidence that sitting children in ability groups of six in primary school helps to close the achievement gap? Why six? Because they fit around the average sized classroom table? Or because that means there is one group for each day of the week?

We know that limited access to language is one of the most significant barriers to learning for disadvantaged children. Where are the great language models when they sit in ability groups?

We know the importance of a growth mindset and children's belief in their ability to learn. What messages do we give to our disadvantaged children when we put them in the 'bottom' group?

Just because 'we've always done it like this' is not a justification for carrying on doing something. Particularly in light of the growing body of evidence that tells us it is wrong!'
Kate Atkins, Rosendale Primary School

Robust Evaluation

Activity is closely monitored at regular milestones for both quality and impact. Changes are made as necessary. Leadership evaluates impact rigorously and unemotionally.

Evaluation should not be about proving that something worked. It's about finding out whether something has worked. This is about cultural change in schools. Finding out about activities that have not worked can be enormously beneficial.

Those involved in Pupil Premium funding activity should be constantly evaluating their impact, and not waiting for milestones if they feel the activity is not working for a particular individual.

Those leading initiatives and activities should be confident in saying 'this isn't working'. Leadership needs to instil a relentless sense of follow up, whatever the activity being evaluated.

Success criteria: Be specific!		
Activity (e.g.)	Treat with caution…	Better!
Additional teacher time to provide specific verbal feedback on areas for improvement	'Improved' end of key stage outcomes / 'Improved' progress	Group of children using responding to verbal feedback in x subject as evidenced in books
Sports activity at the start of the day to improve behavior	Children 'enjoyed' the session	Sustained reduction in the number of behavioural incidents over a given period.
Homework club to improve quality and quantity of homework	Number of pupils signing up	Number of disadvantaged pupils signing up and attending over a period of time. Feedback from teachers that quality and quantity of homework from pupils has improved.
Series of school trips linked to the curriculum as part of enrichment	Improved engagement in lessons 'observed'	Measurable and sustained improvements in the quality of pupil's writing evidenced in books.

Table 5: Be specific with success criteria

A few reminders

- Evaluate quality of process as well as outcome.
- When evaluating, remember to evaluate the process as well as the outcome. Don't just abandon a breakfast club because it hasn't improved attendance. Check whether the breakfast club was any good! This helps prevent school leaders from throwing darts blindly.
- If you only measure the outcome, this target drives everything. It becomes driven by fear of failure rather than enquiry for success.
- Is the commissioning of additional and extra 'time limited' with clear milestones and specific success criteria (not 'I enjoyed!')?
- Are Teaching Assistants confident in saying 'this isn't working?'. Don't wait until the end of an intervention before looking for impact. There should be no surprises at the end.
- Evaluation should not be about proving that something worked. It's about finding out whether something has worked. This is about cultural change in schools. Celebrate a teacher finding out that an initiative has not worked – it means you may save time and energy.
- To evaluate effectively, you have to be clear about what the outcomes will be: Not 'We need to improve attendance' but 'We need to improve attendance by x % by dd/mm by...'
- Outcomes focused... be absolutely clear about what you are trying to achieve – 'improve attainment' is too vague. See Table 5.
- Focus on excellence for pupils – Ofsted judgements are a bi-product. Inspectors are interested in outcomes – not how you do it. But you are unlikely to be judged good or better whilst your disadvantaged learners are attaining poorly.

> '**Knowing who your Pupil Premium children are and what their barriers are is so important. Only then can you begin to think of creative ways to support and help them.**'
>
> Jo Moore, Primary Deputy Headteacher, Buckinghamshire

Part Two

20. What Should I Spend my Pupil Premium on?

It's all about context. In the last two years I have visited about 150 special, primary and secondary schools to learn about their use of the Pupil Premium. These are the active ingredients for success in achieving great outcomes for disadvantaged learners:

- The barriers to learning in the school community are carefully identified. It's much more nuanced that 'you should see the estate many of these pupils come from'.
- Pupil Premium funded activity is appropriate for overcoming these barriers. Activities are carefully planned, delivered with quality and informed by evidence. They are normally time-limited. Objectives are clear, ambitious and tight.
- Activity is closely monitored at regular milestones for both quality and impact. Changes are made as necessary.
- Leadership evaluates impact rigorously and unemotionally.

1. The importance of leadership

This approach is underpinned by *excellent leadership* – have a look at the Ofsted reports for the schools which won Pupil Premium awards in 2014. They demonstrate a strong correlation between closing the gap and great leadership.

Leaders ensure that disadvantaged pupils have a high profile across the school. A light is shone on them and they are expected to attain well. In these schools the Pupil Premium is an important element of the school development plan.

Where other professionals are involved in supporting learners, leaders ensure decision making is joined up with the needs of the pupil. Teachers, leaders and intervention leads agree appropriate action, focused on *gaps in learning* and *not* national curriculum levels. Additional support is exactly that – additional and extra to the teaching in the classroom.

Funding is spent evenly throughout each year group. Schools which intervene and support early, as gaps become evident, are far less likely to be 'cohort vulnerable'.

2. So what *should* I spend my funding on...?

The purpose of the Pupil Premium is to improve attainment for disadvantaged learners. It follows that the funding should be used to ensure these pupils receive consistently excellent teaching.

In some cases, it should be used to maximise *access* to quality first teaching. This may be through intervention programmes such as Reading Recovery, to enable younger children to access the curriculum. It can be transport to school for a young carer. It can be to ensure pupils take part in field trips to provide a richer, more engaging curriculum and better understanding of subsequent class teaching. Wilfred Owen's remarkable poetry has an even greater impact once you have walked the scarred fields of Passchendaele.

Funding can be access to extra-curricular activities to improve attitudes to learning, and it can be breakfast to ensure pupils are not hungry and distracted.

In each case it should be with a very clear purpose – to get pupils learning in the classroom every day through quality first teaching.

3. Spending examples to address a clearly identified need...

- **Slough and Eton CE Business and Enterprise College, Slough:** cultural enrichment for pupils with limited experience of visiting farms, museums in London or other activities, to broaden their horizons and expose them to new thinking.
- **Carwarden House Special School, Surrey:** ICT resources and e-learning to allow pupils with multiple barriers to learning to access the curriculum

- **Stocksbridge Junior School, Sheffield:** training, development and leadership in Kagan cooperative learning to improve speaking and listening during teaching and learning.
- **Woodrow First School, Worcestershire:** family support worker within a community facing particularly challenging circumstances. Also, a relentless focus on oracy to build pupil self-confidence and esteem.

4. More great teaching...

It's simplistic to say 'just get consistently high quality teaching'. Many schools located in challenging communities find recruitment and retention difficult. It is quite appropriate therefore for funding to be used for sustainable approaches to quality teacher recruitment and development. For example:

- Recruitment and retention premiums
- Sabbaticals
- Recruitment of subject/SEN specialists to academy chains or families of schools
- Ongoing, pupil focused CPD
- Additional time for teachers to plan for/evaluate their impact on disadvantaged learners.

In all cases these approaches need to be carried out with a clear focus on what is to be achieved, with follow up, support and resources to ensure objectives are met.

5. Blossoming learners

The Pupil Premium is a wonderfully optimistic policy. It is fertilisation of the possible for learners who have sometimes been allowed to wither through low expectations based on their background.

This article first appeared in Schools Week, January 2015 [36]

21. Ideas to Magpie

Over the past four years across the country – with an appreciative focus on the impact of the Pupil Premium – the National Education Trust has held seminars, conferences and meetings with headteachers, additionally conducting many interviews with pupils and observing significant numbers of classrooms. As an independent foundation we applaud this government initiative, and salute the many ways in which teachers and school leaders are making a real difference to children's and young people's lives through creative, innovative and often exemplary use of the allocated funding.

Reflecting sharply on all that we have seen, we present the following bite sized ideas. This is not a definitive list and we invite readers to add their own recommendations, and share them with us via marc@nationaleducationtrust.net for future editions of this Guide.

- Know what the attainment gap is, how much Pupil Premium funding the school receives, how your school is spending the money, what the impact is, and how you are evaluating for 'next steps'.
- Stop or change course if things are not working.
- Harness your funding to support and stretch higher attainers. Eligibility does not mean low attainment.
- Don't pigeon-hole disadvantaged children as low attainers who are culturally illiterate and disinterested. Ava Sturridge Packer of St Mary's CE Primary School in Birmingham speaks powerfully about children from disadvantaged backgrounds and minority ethnic groups going to the ballet. Enable all children to experience those things perhaps associated with middle-class families.
- Linger over language. The language gap is one of the biggest causes of underachievement in later life, especially for disadvantaged learners. The now famous Hart/Risley

study was published on the impact of language on young children, revealing that low-income children are exposed to 30 million fewer words than their higher-income peers before age three.

- Step back from your school – look up, look out at what other colleagues are doing. Just like a great painting, you'll see your school more clearly from a distance.
- Challenge orthodoxies: children at Level 4c in Year 6 can go to Year 4 for peer tutoring, which improves attainment for younger children and embeds knowledge for older children, with no stigma about 'going back'.
- Go Pupil Premium 'speed dating' with a group of local schools. Hear what people are doing, chose something that interests you, and go and see it.
- Be wary of expensive conferences on Pupil Premium.
- There are no shortcuts or golden tickets! Get your teaching right first.
- Resist the temptation to be 'busy' with your funding.
- If you need to spend your funding on retaining a great teacher, or creating capacity in your leadership team to support, coach and monitor, then spend it there. If you need to improve subject knowledge in Years 3 and 4, so the last two years are not spent catching up, spend it there. Focus on long-term, sustained impact. No Pupil Premium funded activity will be successful if turnover of teaching staff is very high.
- Trust staff, and make them feel trusted. Provide time and space for well-designed research projects which will have a positive impact on pupil outcomes. If the research shows no effect, don't continue down that route. This will create a culture of openness and continuous learning.

- Use the 'Test and Learn' approach for introducing new Pupil Premium funded activities. Supermarkets when introducing a new product will not stack the shelves of every shop in the country. They will introduce carefully – check impact, tweak and change. Once perfected, the product will be rolled out.

- With intervention, look for low effort, high impact. Ask 'can the intervention be sustained?' Louize Allen of the Lambeth Teaching Schools' Alliance talks about the 'Gaudi Test' for interventions and initiatives – will someone value it enough to continue and complete it once you've moved on?

- Self-evaluate regularly. Ask your senior leadership team to write a short report on what Ofsted would say about your school's use of the Pupil Premium. Review this once a term.

- Beware of averages as an outcome. Setting a target of 'average attendance of 95%' for disadvantaged students may mask poor attendance for some children who have very complex barriers to learning. Set your target high for every pupil.

- Focus on progress to improve attainment. A student cannot put on their CV that they got a grade D in GCSE Maths but that they made excellent progress.

- Use funding to enable inexperienced teachers, or those who are struggling, to observe excellent practice. Then coach them for improvement.

- Conduct a skills and subject knowledge audit. Include Teaching Assistants in this process.

- Create time for your team. We have yet to meet a teacher or leader who doesn't value space to read, research or reflect.

- Remember children have hidden talents outside of the classroom. Encourage them to be developed, nurture the privilege of childhood and it might spark something amazing!
- There is no thing as a 'typical' Pupil Premium child. The funding offers a unique opportunity to focus on the individual. Do one size clothes really fit well? A Pupil Premium solution that claims to address the barriers of every learner is likely to be as effective as carrying out surgery with a pneumatic drill.
- The answers to cracking the code for disadvantaged learners doesn't necessarily lie in the Headteacher's office. Get teachers to input into provision. Middle leaders should be championing the cause of disadvantaged learners every day. Parents' views on how to effectively use the funding can be invaluable.
- Don't wait. Use the funding to enable more regular pupil progress meetings. Empower Teaching Assistants to flag up where interventions are not working for a particular child.
- Evidence informed, not evidence led. The EEF Toolkit offers a brilliant opportunity for Pupil Premium activity to be informed by evidence. But it was never intended to be used 'painting by numbers' style. Finding out what works for an individual school context should be closer to independent travel with a guidebook than a coach trip where you are told when and where to get off, when to eat *etc…*
- Get assessment right. If assessment is inconsistent or poor, it is disadvantaged learners who are more likely to 'slip through the net'.
- Monitor progress regularly, evaluate outcomes robustly – but understand that effective quality improvement is not necessarily judgemental.

- Be explicit about what you are trying to achieve and by when. 'Improve numeracy levels' is not clear enough. Hold yourself to account for this.

- Strong values and moral purpose agreed across a whole school are key. Disadvantaged learners need a great experience at school in both structured and unstructured times during the school day. Ensure that disadvantaged learners play a role in wider school life.

- Disadvantaged learners are most successful where teachers in the classroom feel accountable for their outcomes.

- Welcome external input. Working together over a period of time – with colleagues in your cluster or group of schools – can be most valuable. A culture of trust and shared ideas that has grown over time is fundamental importance.

- Be open about data. Teachers should have a clear understanding of how well disadvantaged pupils achieve at a school.

Overcoming the achievement gap is challenging. There are no golden tickets. It requires risk taking and taking people out of comfort zones but, in a system where currently just a third of poorer pupils make the grade, we cannot afford to do nothing.

The Pupil Premium might just be the key that unlocks the opportunity for everyone to attain well.

A Personal Note
Someone recently asked me whether the (under)performance of disadvantaged pupils is a modern phenomenon.

When I was at school, many disadvantaged pupils, and those with special educational needs, were largely put in a 'remedial class'. There they stayed. They were taught by the PE teacher. All the other forms had a name – so in what is now Year 11, there was 5A, 5B... *etc*, you get the idea – and had specialist subject teachers. The remedial classes were called 5'PR'. Apparently this stood for 'progress'.

At lunchtime those eligible for free school meals lined up with their 'dinner token' that screamed 'my parents don't have a job'. This was South Wales in the mid-1980s. A lot of people did not have a job. It was no fault of theirs.

We have more to do to break the link between the cold wind of poverty and educational outcomes, but we have come a long way. The thing our disadvantaged pupils need most is *opportunity*.

PLEASE don't forget the quiet children in the middle. The Pupil Premium is there for them too!

> *'Pupil Premium Plus for children in care can transform lives that have hitherto seemed without hope. Bespoke support for learning helps them grow stronger than the neglect and abuse that put many of them in care in the first place.'*
>
> Mike Gorman, Headteacher, Virtual School for Looked After Children, Bath and North East Somerset

22. Sir John Dunford Interview
Interview with Sir John Dunford, National Pupil Premium Champion 2013-2015

In his role as Pupil Premium champion, John spoke with over 15,000 leaders from Berwick to Boscastle.

1. If you were starting the Pupil Policy from scratch, what would you change?
"It's the best education policy ever, so it should only be changed with great care, if at all. Crucially, politicians aren't telling schools what to do with the money. The Pupil Premium is a high trust, high accountability policy. The simplicity of the policy – with the Pupil Premium paid per child and accountability for impact – is also a strength."

2. Why do high cost – low impact approaches to the Pupil Premium endure?
"I suppose it is because for such a long time we have not been an evidence based profession. GPs have The *BMJ* and *The Lancet*. The Education Endowment Foundation takes us on our first steps towards being more evidence based. The changes we see in the Ofsted Pupil Premium reports mirror changes we have seen in our schools over the past four years. Much of the spending in 2012 was based on 'gut feeling'. In 2015, strategies are far more evidence informed. The EEF's work on Teaching Assistants is particularly useful.

It is worth remembering that even when the evidence is clear, people don't always follow. Using mobile phones whilst driving is a good example."

3. If you were to offer advice to those looking to renew their Pupil Premium strategy, what would you say?
a. Consider the barriers your disadvantaged pupils are facing. No two schools will be the same.
b. Decide upon desired outcomes.

c. Set yourself clear success criteria.
d. Hold yourself to account.
e. Don't look up and expect to be told what to do…"

4. Why are there such wide regional variations in outcomes for disadvantaged learners?

"Fairer funding is an issue, but it is more complex than that. You can make some broad generalisations about the types of LAs that are more successful than others, but weak local leadership is a big issue and there are often big variations in the attainment of disadvantaged children between schools in the same LA."

5. How can the curriculum be a lever for improving outcomes for disadvantaged learners?

"This is a key issue for Whole Education, which I chair. Schools should define their curriculum broadly as 'everything that happens to a child in school' and then plan ways in which skills and personal qualities can be developed alongside knowledge. Making a positive impact on skills development will have a disproportionate benefit for disadvantaged children, who generally have fewer opportunities to develop skills outside school."

6. If you were a Headteacher again, what one thing would you do for disadvantaged learners?

"I would focus very heavily on children who are in care. Their outcomes are horrifying."

October 2015

Part Three

23. Pupil Premium Reviews by the National Education Trust

> *"My wish is that a Pupil Premium review becomes a central part of school improvement"*
>
> David Laws, Minister of State for Schools 2012-2015

Pupil Premium Review
There are a number of resources to support high quality Pupil Premium reviews. Some of those are signposted at the back of this book. This approach has consistently brought about improved outcomes for disadvantaged learners in the schools in which we have worked.

The review process:
- Preparation, document review, self-evaluation and agreeing a schedule for the visit.
- A day in school with feedback to SLT (and anyone else as you see fit) at the end of the day.
- A report will be sent to you. This will analyse current practice and strategy, consider national good practice in relation to the school and provide guidance on action planning, delivery, monitoring and evaluation.
- Guidance will be provided on creating a 'Pupil Premium file' for governors, leaders and inspectors.
- Advice on the school's revised action plan following the review (by correspondence).
- A follow up visit arranged to check on progress, impact if required.

What information is needed ahead of the review?
A paragraph on 'where you feel you are as a school' in respect of the Pupil Premium. Also:

- Any analysis of the expenditure and impact of your current Pupil Premium funding, including how higher attainers eligible for the Pupil Premium achieve.
- Progress and attainment data for Pupil Premium and others in each year group (including any data showing 'gaps within gaps'). This data should include how disadvantaged pupils with SEN are achieving compared with their peers.
- Any analysis of the amount of funding being spent in each year group.
- Any analysis of the major barriers to learning disadvantaged learners face at the school.
- An analysis of the attendance of disadvantaged learners.
- If you are ability grouping, an analysis of which sets disadvantaged pupils are represented in.
- Any analysis of the representation of disadvantaged pupils in extra-curricular activities.

This information received will form the basis of your 'Pupil Premium file' following the review.

On-site visit would include:
- Walk around the school at the start of the day.
- Allocate times for discussions with HT and SLT on arrival.
- Meet with senior leaders, including the SENDCO and subject leaders.
- Speak with those leading Pupil Premium funded work.
- Speak to some of the pupils involved.
- Study examples of marking and feedback in books/folders of disadvantaged pupils.
- Talk with teachers and a governor if possible (even if this is on the telephone).

National Education Trust

Example 1: Pupil Premium Review

PHASE: Primary	RURAL/SEMI URBAN/URBAN:	REGION: South West
OFSTED GRADE: Outstanding	PROPORTION OF DISADVANTAGED LEARNERS: 4.9%	
NOTES:		

Thank you for your time today and for open discussions. The Pupil Premium strategy across both schools is strong. The strategy is more firmly embedded within first school but senior leaders have taken action – including the commissioning of this review – to develop the strategy more thoroughly in the middle school.

The documentation you have produced for the review forms the basis of your Pupil Premium file for governors, inspection, self-review.

Leadership

1. Leadership of the Pupil Premium: A strong message from senior leaders to all staff (including teachers, TAs, midday supervisors) that disadvantaged learners are the highest priority for the school. This message needs to be reiterated regularly.
2. Teachers feeling accountable for the outcomes of disadvantaged learners is key to success with the Pupil Premium. We discussed the self-evaluation question 'if the money was taken away, would disadvantaged pupils at our school still do well'?
3. Part of teacher performance management could link to outcomes for disadvantaged learners.
4. In all cases, expectations for learners should be very high. However, in some very rare cases the key priority may be different – e.g. developing independence.
5. Termly meetings and/or conversations with families of disadvantaged pupils is excellent practice and can be rolled out through the school. This information should be input into your

Pupil Premium record (see 12) so that information and intelligence is shared.

Teaching and Learning

6. Additional marking feedback. It will be well worth trialling an approach to offering additional and extra verbal feedback to disadvantaged learners. This should be done systematically and be evaluated following a trial period.
7. Ability grouping: We had an extended conversation about moving away from ability grouping (more about this here: https://educationendowmentfoundation.org.uk/toolkit/toolkit-a-z/ability-grouping/) and how this can negatively impact on outcomes for disadvantaged pupils. With coaching, monitoring and support, a move to mixed ability teaching in Year 5 would be a positive move. We also discussed a staged move to 'banding' in Year 6 – with a higher, middle and emerging group. This would be supported by joint planning. Moving away from ability grouping will fit positively with the new national curriculum.

Additional and Extra (including Intervention)

8. Every intervention should have clearly identified, time limited outcomes that are monitored and evaluated. It is important to avoid the 'year of one to one'.
9. Parent's evenings: These might be pupil led to build ownership of learning and improve parental engagement.
10. We discussed the possibility of phase groups/year groups being given a small proportion of Pupil Premium funding for researching approaches to raising attainment for disadvantaged pupils. Groups should present their research to teaching staff.
11. The **Catch Up Numeracy** programme may fit well with requirements in middle school. More here: https://education endowmentfoundation.org.uk/projects/catch-up-numeracy/

Monitoring and Evaluation

12. A merger of the 'vulnerable groups' document and 'progress and attainment' document. A single central record for all disadvantaged and vulnerable learners that includes: achievement, barriers,

additional and extra support, success criteria and monitoring/evaluation.
13. This record should be updated at regular milestones and class teachers should input into this record.
14. All Pupil Premium children should remain on the register, regardless of whether they are actively vulnerable, or just dormant.
15. Pupils should be differentiated by FSM, ever6, Forces, LAC.
16. Every pupil should receive some additional and extra if they are eligible for funding. But the Pupil Premium should not be considered a fixed per pupil alliance.
17. It should include an agreed 'non negotiables' agreed by the school e.g. an opportunity to learn a musical instrument.
18. Attendance and punctuality should also be closely monitored, as should children's participation in wider school life.
19. This record avoids repetition of interventions unnecessarily and ensures information is not lost during transition. We discussed the need to be sharper in terms of information gathering during transition from other schools, and of passing information on when children go to new schools. Disadvantaged pupils should, where appropriate, be entitled to extended transition arrangements.
20. Model Pupil Premium statements can be found at the following schools:
http://www.stocksbridge-jun.sheffield.sch.uk/sjs-information/pupil-premium (I like the regularity of updates).
http://www.steugene.camden.sch.uk/sites/default/files/u8/St%20Eugene%27s%20Impact%20of%20Pupil%20Premium%20Funding%202013-2014%20for%20webs.pdf (I like the simplicity and clarity of this one).

National Education Trust

Example 2: Pupil Premium Review

PHASE: Primary	RURAL/SEMI URBAN/URBAN:	REGION: East
OFSTED GRADE: Good	PROPORTION OF DISADVANTAGED LEARNERS: 16.2%	
NOTES:		

475 O/R	The School has recently had some mixed results for its disadvantaged learners, with a significant gap between those children and their more advantaged peers in achieving L4+ RWM in 2014. In 2015, there looks to be an improvement at the end of KS2, and KS1 results look good for all children. Despite this, the school remains 'cohort vulnerable'.
28.8% Pupil Premium	
16.2% FSM	
5.3% SEN	
14.4% EAL	

Thank you for inviting me to your school today and for the open and honest discussions.

Leadership

1. Senior leadership commissioned this review having reflected that the school's current strategy could be improved so that the pupil premium has greater impact on the disadvantaged learners the school serves. This is clearly a renewed priority for the SLT who are looking to take prompt action. *We will review actions against this report in the autumn term 2015.*

2. Some time needs to be spent reiterating that tackling educational disadvantage is a key priority for the school. Every member of school staff, teaching and non-teaching, should be working to ensure that the school is a great place to learn if you come from a disadvantaged background.

3. Senior Leadership had a very clear understanding of the barriers disadvantaged pupils faced. These included reading, attitudes to learning, parental engagement, attendance/punctuality and oracy. In some cases it was acknowledged that the barrier has been inconsistent teaching and learning.

An Updated Practical Guide to the Pupil Premium

4. Data on children eligible for the pupil premium needs to be more secure. There is good knowledge of which children are in receipt of funding but this information does not always marry up with in-school databases.
5. The website statement needs to provide a clearer story about how the school is using the pupil premium effectively. See the following examples:

   http://www.steugene.camden.sch.uk/sites/default/files/u8/St%20Eugene%27s%20Impact%20of%20Pupil%20Premium%20Funding%202013-2014%20for%20webs.pdf

   http://www.stocksbridge-jun.sheffield.sch.uk/sjs-information/pupil-premium (look at the 9 November update)

6. Audit: carry out a termly audit to ensure you a) have a live 'one stop shop' of the barriers children are facing, and also the Pupil Premium funded activities they are receiving to overcome those barriers. This will help you show that *all* children in receipt of the funding are targeted, including your higher attainers. The INCO role should be to oversee this, not complete it. Include a 'last reviewed' date one it.
7. Your Pupil Premium data file should include all the documents set out in the pre-review template. We discussed that the principles of good leadership for SEND children apply to pupil premium. The overarching strategy should be reviewed termly by the SLT.
8. We had a detailed discussion about effective monitoring and evaluation. In particular, we agreed that the purpose of regular monitoring is to ensure quality improvement and 'no surprises' at the end of Pupil Premium funded activity. We also agreed that success criteria should be specifically linked to the issues any activity was trying to address e.g. attendance, self-esteem, specific gaps in learning rather than National Curriculum Levels or other overarching outcomes.

Teaching and Learning

9. During the review we had a general discussion about the strengths and weaknesses of teaching across the school, and how this had a disproportionate impact in disadvantaged learners.

10. We agreed that more needed to be done to ensure that all teachers need to feel accountable for their disadvantaged pupils' outcomes.
11. We particularly focused in on strategies to improve the quality and impact of marking and feedback. I understand that some work is going on to improve this across the school, but we discussed how particularly important high quality feedback is to disadvantaged learners.
12. During the review we agreed that SLT would agree a strategy to allow additional time for teachers twice a week to feed back to their disadvantaged learners. This would also provide feedback to teachers themselves about children's learning.
13. We agreed to trial this approach in two year groups before any role out across the school takes place.
14. 'Book looks': Again, to increase the focus on disadvantaged pupils in the school, SLT will (at fixed points) gather in books of disadvantaged pupils across years to check on progress and the impact of feedback.
15. We received data for the outcomes of disadvantaged pupils across each year group and considered how Pupil Premium funding could support any CPD needs for teachers. Any Pupil Premium funded CPD should only be commissioned with clearly identified outcomes for disadvantaged learners.
16. Teachers need to play a greater role in the commissioning of additional and extra support through intervention. Intervention should not be a first resort but a carefully considered process, ideally using a Pupil Premium 'bidding' form. It is important that teachers themselves feel accountable for pupil outcomes.
17. The school uses the *catch up* programme, which is very positive given the strong evidence base that sits behind it, and how it encourages the effective use of TAs.

Family Support Worker
18. This role was identified as a strength in the current Pupil Premium strategy. In particular, the positive relations built between disadvantaged families and their schools, starting with a home visit. However, there needs to be more done to greater clarity about the impact/outcomes this role will have. Further, the

information gathered in this role needs to feed into leadership intelligence and Pupil Premium provision mapping. Steps are being taken to ensure these things are in place for 2015/16.

Attendance

19. During the review we dug deep into attendance. We discussed a refocus on improving attendance across the school, but particularly for disadvantaged pupils whose attendance and punctuality was poorer that their peers.
20. We agreed that a focus on the attendance on individual pupils, rather than 'average', as very good or very poor attendance from a small number of individuals masks problems.
21. A whole school strategy is required to tackle the issue, which may be linked to some of the primary barriers to learning such as parental engagement and poor attitudes. This should start at Governor Level, highlighting what is expected as a non-negotiable. Then this is followed up by senior leaders, at class level and also by family support. This strategy should include positive and punitive approaches where appropriate. Set some very clear and ambitious targets with clear milestones. It would also be helpful to gather together a small focus group of families to ask what could help them improve their children's attendance.
22. We discussed that any extrinsic incentives for attendance should be awarded to all that meet thresholds.
23. A breakfast club is currently in place but that tends to serve other children rather than those that are disadvantaged. Some careful targeting of families through the Family Support worker may prove effective.

Wider School Life

24. It was agreed that a sharper focus on the extent to which disadvantaged learners are taking part in wider school life is required.

An Updated Practical Guide to the Pupil Premium

National Education Trust

Example 3: Pupil Premium Review

PHASE: Primary	RURAL/SEMI URBAN/URBAN:	REGION: North
OFSTED GRADE: Outstanding	PROPORTION OF DISADVANTAGED LEARNERS: 16.2%	
NOTES:		

In summary:
The performance of disadvantaged learners at the end of Key Stage 2 outstrips local and national levels significantly in 2014:

KS2 Results RWM Combined: L4B+ (Pupil Premium Only)

School: 83%
LA: 49%
England: 53%

Visit:
Disadvantaged children do well because excellence is considered standard at the school. High expectations and consistency are explicit everywhere, as are the school's values in the classrooms and the corridors.

The Pupil Premium 'works' at the school because it is closely aligned with the overarching development plans. During the visit we had the opportunity to see very high quality teaching and learning across the school which (as evidence shows) has a disproportionate impact on disadvantaged learners.

The school community has a very clear reflection of its values and expectations. This is evidenced from the welcome on arrival, to teaching with open doors, to the confidence disadvantaged children with multiple barriers have, in discussing their learning with visitors.

The Action Research:
1. **Raise attainment for all Pupil Premium children**, with

success criteria identified as rapid progress and (crucially) staff accountable for the disadvantaged children in their class. The focus, importantly, is on the gaps in learning, rather than the 'level'. In this action research project, the priority to raise attainment is tackled through introduction of assertive mentoring for Pupil Premium children in reading, writing and maths.
2. **Extend the school day** to provide consistency in quality teaching and to allow pupil premium children to attend booster classes, clubs and use technology.
   This plan to tackle this priority is through Year 6 booster classes, learning opportunities at the start of the day and a high quality homework club.
3. All children to display a **positive attitude to learning and school life**.
   This priority is tackled through the 'pupil support role', opportunities for disadvantaged learners to prioritise interests and important focus on improving attendance.
4. Developing management strategies that create a **sustainable** approach to **parent partnership**.
5. This work builds on Sheffield's LPPA.

For each project strand, a clear programme of aim, activity (with a person responsible), monitoring and impact evaluation is in place.

There is good evidence to show that each of these strands are showing a positive impact. As expected, this evidence varies by strand as they address complex issues. What is powerful is the adaptability of approaches – through monitoring and evidence, it has been possible to change course where necessary. An example is the changes in approaches to homework.

Involving other leaders to play a role in the school's approach to narrowing the gap, both in terms of strategy and operation, is crucial in embedding success.

> *The school's work will form a crucial part of the action research dissemination. A strong argument can be made to say that [more] robust evidence of impact of action research is being seen because of the sense of organisation, clarity of expectation and vision that is evident throughout the school.*
>
> *Even better if... to think about how Year 3 teachers could hit the ground running with disadvantaged pupils by having greater prior knowledge of children's strengths, weaknesses and support they have already received.*

During the visit, we also considered the wider benefits of the project:
- Collaboration and partnership, both in terms of the research relationship with, and the wider group of school in the project).
- Good practice (eg Kagan, Impact Evaluation).
- The visit/review process which has also mean that some of the strengths seen at the school could be shared with others during other visits.

Please say thank you again to all staff and pupils for such a warm welcome.

National Education Trust

Example 4: Pupil Premium Review

PHASE: Secondary	RURAL/SEMI URBAN/URBAN: Urban	REGION: London
OFSTED GRADE: Outstanding	PROPORTION OF DISADVANTAGED LEARNERS: 7.8%	
NOTES:		

Thank you for the very warm welcome and the open and honest discussions today.

The main purpose of the visit was to support more effective impact evaluation of Pupil Premium funded activity.

I met with the Headteacher, senior and middle leaders as part of the day. We reviewed previous activity/impact and considered how things might evolve ahead.

We discussed some of the successes of the school's current Pupil Premium strategy – for example the Family Liaison Officers, roles. And also considered plans to make further changes ahead – for example efforts to focus on 'filling in cracks early rather than trying to bridge crevasses later on' and the role of Assistant Head of Year to play a lead role in Pupil Premium in each year group.

We also discussed the primary barriers to learning the school's disadvantaged pupils face.

Notes from the visit:

Teaching and Intervention

1. The key to success in narrowing the gap is for teachers in the classroom to feel accountable for the outcomes of disadvantaged learners.
2. Where intervention is required, it should be additional and extra to a 'diet' of consistent excellent teaching that meets the needs of individual learners.
3. Teachers should be involved in the commissioning of such additional

and extra intervention. It should be strictly time limited with very specific success criteria which enables you to measure success.
4. Where possible, those leading interventions should be confident about flagging up a) where intervention is no longer needed and b) where it is not appropriate. It is important not to wait for milestones in some cases.
5. This activity should be monitored and evaluated at SLT level. The key to success with any intervention is being *very specific* about the success criteria. Requests for intervention should be rejected if this is absent or incomplete.
6. We considered options for base lining Year 7s. The key issue here is reminding Year 7 teachers that it is more likely that disadvantaged pupils will slip back after SATs, the summer break and when moving into Year 7.
7. A focus on 'Level 4cs' is important. The 'catch up numeracy' programme has a good evidence base for those pupils that are not attaining at age related expectations by Year 7. It is led by TAs. More details here: www.catchup.org/CatchUpNumeracy/CatchUpNumeracy.aspx
8. We discussed the importance of high quality, trained TAs that can effectively work with disadvantaged and vulnerable learners.
9. In subjects where there is ability grouping, consider where your disadvantaged pupils are over represented and what movement there is between sets. This is something that could be monitored at curriculum leader level (who will be accountable to SLT). Boosters for disadvantaged pupils (and others) that are higher attainers may be appropriate.
10. The marking and feedback of disadvantaged learners' work is highly important. As discussed, this may well be the only feedback they receive on their work. Therefore, regular reviews of how marking and feedback *moves forward* the learning of disadvantaged learners is key to success, and keeps these learners at the top of the agenda.

Leadership

11. We had an extended discussion about the Assistant Head of Year role and their key role in improving outcomes for disadvantaged learners. Their responsibilities will include areas such as attendance and punctuality, parental engagement, FLOs, Above and Beyond. These should be accountable to SLT but, again, should be flagging up concerns before review meetings.
12. At a senior leadership level, I think it would be useful to be regularly self-evaluating the effectiveness of the Pupil Premium strategy. Ideally this should take place half termly and be presented to governors. It enables you to lead the agenda and tell the story of your Pupil Premium strategy should you receive visits from inspectors. Keep this to a side of A4.
13. Include progress and attainment for each year group (not overly focusing on KS4) and record whether the expenditure of pupil premium is proportionate to the numbers of disadvantaged learners in each year group.

And finally…

14. I think there is much to feel positive about in respect of the actions undertaken to tackle educational disadvantage at the school.
15. The next steps feel very much on the right track – to put tackling underachievement by disadvantaged learners at the top of the agenda at a strategic level. But the key to success in tackling educational inequality is owned by every staff member in the school, particularly those teachers in the classroom.
16. I am very happy to return to talk to staff about Pupil Premium and work through some practical steps.

National Education Trust

Example 5: Pupil Premium Review

PHASE: Secondary	RURAL/SEMI URBAN/URBAN: Urban	REGION: London
OFSTED GRADE: Good	PROPORTION OF DISADVANTAGED LEARNERS: 15.3%	
NOTES:		

Leadership

1. The leadership of the Pupil Premium is strong. Data analysis and tracking is forensic in its detail, with actions agreed against that data analysis.
2. Performance data for both disadvantaged learners and their peers looks very promising for 2015, with a trend of improving attainment for all learners. Disadvantaged learners are on track to outperform their disadvantaged peers nationally, within the LA and at a level of some of the highest performing LAs in the country.

An additional analysis of how disadvantaged pupils with SEN and their disadvantaged peers may inform greater targeting or resources and understanding of gaps within gaps.

3. Leadership capacity is given over to plan a very clear, coherent and well-resourced strategy to improve outcomes for disadvantaged learners.
4. There is a well-organised, well-resourced plan that is being trialled to better understand the barriers to learning.
5. Improving academic outcomes through great teaching with the foundation stones in place for great learning.
6. The model takes the very best primary practice and places a system where that can be replicated within the more complex challenges of the secondary sector.

Be clear to articulate that whilst the focus on knowledge and understanding of barriers young people face, improving relationships, self-esteem are in order to improve academic outcomes, rather than instead of...

7. Accounting. Keep this simple. The use of funding does not need to be allocated to the penny to each student. That said, there should be a process that ensures that every learner from a disadvantaged background is targeted with some additional and extra resource as per their needs. Equality of opportunity is not equality of provision.
8. In respect of evaluation focus on: a) the impact of a given initiative on a learner – '*has metacognition improved outcomes for pupil A*', b) the trends that come out of any initiative – '*has metacognition improved outcomes for this group of 35 pupils?*' and c) '*Is metacognition of high quality and good value for money?*'
9. Middle leaders are clear about the schools' strategy to improve outcomes. There has been a sharpening of focus so there is absolutely clarity over what the overstaffing of year groups achieves for disadvantaged learners. This is being carefully tracked and monitored.
10. Evaluate the impact of any initiative on the basis that it achieves what you want it to achieve, rather than on its impact on NC levels/predicted GCSE grades.
11. Systems are in place in Maths to ensure consistently good teachers are recruited and retained in to the department.
12. The work to improve relationships between pupils and teachers digs deep to create sustained, long term impact. The aim is to ensure this approach is embedded across the school – a process of cultural change.

I would recommend that this cultural change process is reiterated regularly to all staff, to reinforce the message that early intervention and strong relationships lead to better academic outcomes.

13. The Pupil Premium working group can be the engine room in driving this message across the school. *Be sure to include some sceptics on your working group!*
14. Governance is strong, knowledgeable and well informed, with

regular and open updates and information received. Strong relationships underpinned by trust are fundamental.

My challenge to SLT is to be wary of expending all energies on lots of great things. At a leadership level, perhaps cap interventions and initiatives to a manageable amount – based on what is most effective. This focuses the mind on robust evaluation.

Secondly, in respect of the Pupil Premium, the breadth and depth of the work may mean that all student outcomes improve, your ambition should focus on a trend of narrowing the gap within the context of an overall improvement in attainment. However, it is better to have 60% PP/75% Other than 55% across the board. Ask, is this a great school to go to if you come from a disadvantaged background?

15. In your Pupil Premium mapping, check that your higher attainers are being suitably targeted with funds to enable them to do even better and/or sustain success.

Pupils

16. Behaviour around the school is very good. There is creativity about the school environment. The welcome on reception is very warm and positive. This is very important seen through the eyes of a disadvantaged learner.
17. Pupils are confident and articulate in talking about their perceptions of the schools' strengths and weaknesses. They are able to make credible suggestions about what would make the school even better. They are very confident about this and I very much enjoyed our discussion.

Students talked about issues around self-esteem of knowing they are in a low set. How these sets are labelled could be considered further. Also, whether timetabling issues mean that you are placed in a low set due to underperformance in another subject area needs further thought.

Carry out a general review of which sets disadvantaged pupils are represented in.

Might Pupil Premium be used to improve behaviour management in lower sets?

18. The passports model is excellent practice. SLT needs to monitor that these are acted upon as they are rolled out across the school.
19. The work to improve children's metacognitive skills can be powerful. It is being well researched and, if done effectively, will link closely to the school's overarching strategy to improve outcomes for all. This is being well led, but it is no quick fix.
20. The personalised approach – transport, alarm clocks etc – to ensure young people are accessing quality first teaching is powerful.

Consider how much the extracurricular provision the school is making benefits disadvantaged learners. Carry out a sharp analysis of this.

Consider a pupil forum that represents disadvantaged learners and their experience of schools. You could consider something similar for parents. See the school through the eyes of some of your disadvantaged families. How could it be even better?

21. The lesson I observed modelled a much personalised approach, challenging pupils with high expectations through a model that focused on individual levers. The teacher cleverly scaffolded what to do using models from pupils' prior learning, reinforcing what they were capable of and signposting where to go next.

Consider a pilot of pupils leading parent consultations – taking ownership of learning, apathy.

Consider whether there could be an arts project that specifically targets disadvantaged learners.

Strengths
- Personalisation
- Targeting
- Whole school strategy
- Test and learn
- T&L
- Tracking for a purpose

Challenges
- Manageability (admin). It is quite appropriate to use Pupil Premium to manage admin to improve leadership capacity.

- Don't get bogged down in trying to evaluate the impact of a trip to university. Evaluate the package of raising aspirations. Did we achieve what we wanted to achieve.
- Numbers of interventions – are there too many?
- Disadvantaged higher attainers – a clearer strategy needed.
- Ensure that the purpose of personalisation is explicit – it is about creating great outcomes, not instead of. Set yourself some rigorous targets for academic achievement of disadvantaged pupils in each year group.

22. Clearly lots of hard work – with significant impact – has taken place over a short space of time. Congratulations to all. The next step is to tighten up in a way that sustainably sustains these successes.

Part Four

24. Ofsted Guidance – Analysis and Challenge Tools for Schools[37]

Analysis and challenge toolkit for school leaders: secondary	**128**
Where are the Gaps in Year 11?	129
Where are the Gaps (other Year Groups)?	130
Where are the Gaps (other Eligible Groups)?	130
Reflective Questions	130
Analysis and challenge toolkit for school leaders: primary	**131**
Where are the Gaps (Year 6)?	132
Where are the Gaps (other Year Groups)?	133
Where are the Gaps (other Eligible Groups)?	133
Reflective Questions	133
Planning and evaluation outline	**134**
Self-review questions for governing bodies	**135**

Analysis and Challenge Toolkit for School Leaders: Secondary

On the following pages are modified versions of the tables used by inspectors during the Pupil Premium survey. Schools could use these to inform discussions between school leaders and governors, and help to shape future strategic planning for the use of the Pupil Premium funding. The tools could also be used to aid self-evaluation and may help with preparing for a Section 5 or Section 8 inspection. The tables can be adapted for future use by changing the dates. They could also be adapted to focus on achievement gaps for any other groups in the school.

Data for the pupil outcomes table for Year 11 should be taken from RAISEonline.

Data for other year groups should be available from the school's own tracking of pupils' attainment and progress.

Financial year	Amount of Pupil Premium funding
2011-12	
2012-13	
2013-14	

	2011-12		2012-13
Percentage of FSM pupils			
Number of FSM pupils eligible for the Pupil Premium	@£488	=	@£623
Number of looked after pupils eligible for the Pupil Premium	@£488	=	@£623
Number of service children eligible for the Pupil Premium	@£200	=	@£250
Total			

Where are the Gaps in Year 11?

Year 11: Indicator (using data from RAISEonline for 2011 and 2012, and school data for current Year 11. Definition of FSM for this purpose is the same as RAISE – those pupils eligible for the Pupil Premium under the 'Ever 6' measure. LAC and service children in later section).	2011 gap between FSM and non FSM	2012 gap between FSM and non FSM	2013 predicted outcome for FSM	2013 predicted outcome for non FSM	2013 predicted gap	Comments/ contextual information
Attainment – 5+ A*-C passes including English and mathematics						
Attainment – average points score in English						
Attainment – average points score in mathematics						
Attainment – average points score (best eight GCSEs)						
Attainment – average points score (best eight GCSEs including equivalents)						
Achievement – expected progress in English						
Achievement – more than expected progress in English						
Achievement – expected progress in mathematics						
Achievement – more than expected progress in mathematics						
Achievement – value-added score (best eight GCSEs)						
Achievement – value-added score (best eight GCSEs including equivalents)						
Attendance						
Persistent absence						
Fixed-term exclusions						

Where are the Gaps (other Year Groups)?

Year group	What does your data analysis tell you about the relative attainment and achievement of FSM and non-FSM pupils for each year group? Are there any gaps? To what extent are gaps closing compared with previous years' data?
Year 7	
Year 8	
Year 9	
Year 10	

Where are the Gaps (other Eligible Groups)?

Group	Comment on predicted outcomes in 2013 and any gaps. Consider attainment, progress, attendance and exclusions.
Looked after children	
Service children	

Reflective Questions

To what extent are the strengths and priorities suggested by this data clearly evident in the school's self-evaluation and improvement plans? If any are missing, outline them below and add them to your improvement plan, or use the separate planning and evaluation outline on page 133.
Which strengths are not reflected in your self-evaluation?
Which priorities are not reflected in your school improvement plans?

Analysis and Challenge Toolkit for School Leaders: Primary

On the following pages are modified versions of the tables used by inspectors during the Pupil Premium survey. Schools could use these to inform discussions between school leaders and governors, and help to shape future strategic planning for the use of the Pupil Premium funding. The tools could also be used to aid self-evaluation and may help with preparing for a Section 5 or Section 8 inspection. The tables can be adapted for future use by changing the dates. They could also be adapted to focus on achievement gaps for any other groups in the school.

Data for the pupil outcomes table for Year 6 should be taken from RAISEonline.
Data for other year groups should be available from the school's own tracking of pupils' attainment and progress.

Financial year	Amount of Pupil Premium funding
2011-12	
2012-13	
2013-14	

	2013-14		2014-15	
Percentage of FSM pupils				
Number of FSM pupils eligible for the Pupil Premium	@£	=	@£	=
Number of looked after pupils eligible for the Pupil Premium	@£	=	@£	=
Number of service children eligible for the Pupil Premium	@£	=	@£	=
Total				

Where are the Gaps (Year 6)?

Year 6: Indicator (using data from RAISEonline for 2011 and 2012, and school data for current Year 6. Definition of FSM for this purpose is the same as RAISE – those pupils eligible for the Pupil Premium under the 'Ever6' measure. LAC and service children in later section).	2013 gap between FSM and non FSM	2013 gap between FSM and non FSM	2014 predicted outcome for FSM	2014 predicted outcome for non FSM	2014 predicted gap	Comments/ contextual information
Attainment – Level 4+ in English						
Attainment – Level 4+ in mathematics						
Average points score – English						
Average points score – reading						
Average points score – writing						
Average points score – mathematics						
Achievement – expected progress in English						
Achievement – more than expected progress in English						
Achievement – expected progress in mathematics						
Achievement – more than expected progress in mathematics						
Attendance						
Persistent absence						
Fixed-term exclusions						

Where are the Gaps (other Year Groups)?

Year group	What does your data analysis tell you about the relative attainment and achievement of FSM and non-FSM pupils for each year group? Are there any gaps? Is there evidence of closing gaps compared with previous years' data?
Early Years Foundation Stage	
Year 1 (consider whether pupils are making expected progress on the basis of their Early Years Foundation Stage score; consider the phonics screening check)	
Year 2 (consider predicted end of Key Stage results for reading, writing and mathematics at each sub-level, as well as current data)	
Year 3	
Year 4	
Year 5	

Where are the Gaps (other Eligible Groups)?

Group	Comment on predicted outcomes in 2013 and any gaps. Consider attainment, progress, attendance and exclusions.
Looked after children	
Service children	

Reflective Questions

To what extent are the strengths and priorities suggested by this data clearly evident in the school's self-evaluation and improvement plans? If any are missing, outline them below and add them to your improvement plan or use the separate planning and evaluation outline on p133.
Which strengths are not reflected in your self-evaluation?
Which priorities are not reflected in your school improvement plans?

Planning and evaluation outline

Pupil Premium used for:	Amount allocated to the intervention / action (£)	Is this a new or continued activity/cost centre?	Brief summary of the intervention or action, including details of year groups and pupils involved, and the timescale	Specific intended outcomes: how will this intervention or action improve achievement for pupils eligible for the Pupil Premium? What will it achieve if successful?	How will this activity be monitored, when and by whom? How will success be evidenced?	Actual impact: What did the action or activity actually achieve? Be specific: 'As a result of this action...' If you plan to repeat this activity, what would you change to improve it next time?

Self-review questions for Governing Bodies
Governors' knowledge and awareness
1. Have leaders and governors considered research and reports about what works to inform their decisions about how to spend the Pupil Premium?
2. Do governors know how much money is allocated to the school for the Pupil Premium? Is this identified in the school's budget planning?
3. Is there a clearly understood and shared rationale for how this money is spent and what it should achieve? Is this communicated to all stakeholders including parents?
4. Do governors know how the school spends this money? What improvements has the allocation brought about? How is this measured and reported to governors and parents via the school's website (a new requirement)?
5. If this funding is combined with other resources, can governors isolate and check on the impact of the funding and ascertain the difference it is making?
6. Do governors know whether leaders and managers are checking that the actions are working and are of suitable quality?

Leaders and managers' actions
1. Do the school's improvement/action plans identify whether there are any issues in the performance of pupils who are eligible for the Pupil Premium?
2. Do the actions noted for improving outcomes for Pupil Premium pupils:
    - give details of how the resources are to be allocated?
    - give an overview of the actions to be taken?
    - give a summary of the expected outcomes?
    - identify ways of monitoring the effectiveness of these actions as they are ongoing and note who will be responsible for ensuring that this information is passed to governors?
    - explain what will be evaluated at the end of the action and what measures of success will be applied?

3. Is the leader responsible for this area of the school's work identified?
4. How do governors keep an ongoing check on these actions and ask pertinent questions about progress ahead of any summary evaluations?
5. Are the progress and outcomes of eligible pupils identified and analysed by the school's tracking systems? Is this information reported to governors in a way that enables them to see clearly whether the gap in the performance of eligible pupils and other pupils is closing?

Pupils' progress and attainment
1. Does the summary report of RAISEonline show that there are any gaps in performance between pupils who are eligible for free school meals and those who are not at the end of key stages? (Look at the tables on the previous pages of this document for some indicators to consider)
2. Do the school's systems enable governors to have a clear picture of the progress and attainment of pupils who are eligible for the Pupil Premium **in all year groups across the school**, not just those at the end of key stages?
3. If there are gaps in the attainment of pupils who are eligible for the Pupil Premium and those who are not, are eligible pupils making accelerated progress – are they progressing faster than the expected rate – in order to allow the gaps to close? Even if all pupils make expected progress this will not necessarily make up for previous underperformance.
4. Is the school tracking the attendance, punctuality and behaviour (particularly exclusions) of this group and taking action to address any differences?

Overall, will governors know and be able to intervene quickly if outcomes are not improving in the way that they want them to?

Part Five

25. Acknowledgements

With thanks to...

The great joy in this work has been sharing effective practice and effective process which, in a small way, helps schools do even better for their disadvantaged learners.

I would like to thank all those schools which opened their doors to me as I researched this book. I have tried hard to acknowledge those that have contributed.

I am grateful for the open and honest discussions that were had throughout. Special thanks to everyone at Rosendale primary school for answering my endless questions, and to everyone at Limpsfield Grange Special School, a reminder of what can be done against the odds.

I would also like say a big thank you to the following for their help, advice and insights:

Kate Atkins
Roy Blatchford
Liz Bramley
Lucy Crehan
Steve Davies
Sir John Dunford
Sam Gaymond
Mike Gorman
Simon Knight
Stefano Pozzi
Pam Smith
Chris Wood HMI

Finally, I'd like to thank Kate Cheshire (editor) for having the patience of an emperor penguin.

Marc Rowland

26. Further Reading

The main page of *The EEF Toolkit*, with the strategies in order of effectiveness http://educationendowmentfoundation.org.uk/toolkit/

Page 3 of the Ofsted report on PP (Feb 2013), which summarised the successful and unsuccessful approaches to using Pupil Premium https://www.gov.uk/government/publications/the-pupil-premium-how-schools-are-spending-the-funding-successfully

The report on the Deployment and Impact of Support Staff (DISS) project on Teaching Assistants at www.oxfordprimary.co.uk: http://fdslive.oup.com/www.oup.com/oxed/primary/literacy/osi_teaching_assistants_report_web.pdf?region=uk

Ofsted resource on evaluation of Pupil Premium effectiveness https://www.gov.uk/government/publications/the-pupil-premium-analysis-and-challenge-tools-for-schools

Article for middle leaders from the Spring 2014 of *Teaching Leaders Quarterly*: http://www.teachingleaders.org.uk/wp-content/uploads/2014/03/TL_Quarterly_Q5_14_Dunford.pdf

Blogs: *Ten Point Plan on Spending the Pupil Premium successfully* http://johndunfordconsulting.wordpress.com/ and summary (September 2015)

Education Endowment Foundation tool for comparing Pupil Premium performance of each secondary school within its family of 50 most-like schools http://educationendowmentfoundation.org.uk/toolkit/families-of-schools/ (primary school version to be published March 2015)

Guidance on conducting Pupil Premium reviews. Also useful for doing school self-review of PP strategies (published December 2014) http://tscouncil.org.uk/guide-effective-pupil-premium-reviews/

Sheffield Pupil Premium Action Research Group *Tackling Education Disadvantage by Understanding What Works*. National Education Trust/Sheffield LA (2015) http://www.nationaleducationtrust.net/Downloads/SheffieldPupilPremiumARG.pdf

Ofsted report on *Unseen Children* http://www.ofsted.gov.uk/resources/unseen-children-access-and-achievement-20-years

A link to the Free School Meals toolkit, which give practical ideas for increasing registration. http://www.childrensfoodtrust.org.uk/resources/fsm/free-school-meals-matter-toolkit

National Audit Office report on Pupil Premium (June 2015) http://www.nao.org.uk/report/funding-for-disadvantaged-pupils/

House of Commons – Funding for Disadvantaged Pupils, Committee of Public Accounts (July 2015) http://data.parliament.uk/writtenevidence/committeeevidence.svc/evidencedocument/public-accounts-committee/funding-for-disadvantaged-pupils/oral/18774.html

Equality and Human Rights Commission. *Creating a Fairer Britain*. http://www.equalityhumanrights.com/largest-ever-review-reveals-%E2%80%98winners-and-losers%E2%80%99-progress-towards-equality-great-britain

https://www.gov.uk/government/uploads/system/uploads/attachment_data/file/473974/DFE-RR411_Supporting_the_attainment_of_disadvantaged_pupils.pdf

27. References

1. Professor Derek Bell. *Beyond Show and Tell*. Retrieved from http://www.nationaleducationtrust.net/SchoolImprovementServices/beyondShowAndTell/ShowAndTellDownload.pdf
2. Marc Rowland. *Special Education for the Next Generation, A Collection of Essays*. Retrieved from http://www.nationaleducationtrust.net/Resources/SpecialEducation.pdf
3. Equality and Human Rights Commission. *Creating a Fairer Britain*. Retrieved from http://www.equalityhumanrights.com/largest-ever-review-reveals-%E2%80%98winners-and-losers%E2%80%99-progress-towards-equality-great-britain
4. Anthony Lord, Jenny Easby & Helen Evans, Department for Education. Pupils not claiming Free School Meals Research Report (2013). Retrieved from https://www.gov.uk/government/uploads/system/uploads/attachment_data/file/266339/DFE-RR319.pdf
5. Department for Education. *Pupil Premium Awards*. Retrieved from http://www.pupilpremiumawards.co.uk/
6. Hammond Academy. Retrieved from www.hammondacademy.org.uk/88/pupil-premium
7. Sheffield Pupil Premium Action Research Group *Tackling Education Disadvantage by Understanding What Works*. National Education Trust/Sheffield LA (2015) Retrieved from http://www.nationaleducationtrust.net/Downloads/SheffieldPupilPremiumARG.pdf
8. Department for Education. Early Years Pupil Premium Guide. Retrieved from https://www.gov.uk/guidance/early-years-pupil-premium-guide-for-local-authorities
9. Education Endowment Foundation. *Early Years Toolkit*. Retrieved from https://educationendowmentfoundation.org.uk/toolkit
10. Education Endowment Foundation. *Making the Best Use of Teaching Assistants*. Retrieved from https://educationendowmentfoundation.org.uk/uploads/pdf/TA_Guidance_Report_Interactive.pdf
11. Webster, R., Russell, A. and Blatchford, P. (2016) *Maximising the Impact of Teaching Assistants: Guidance for School Leaders and Teachers*. Second edition, Oxon: Routledge

12. Bosanquet, P., Radford, J. and Webster, R. (2016) *The Teaching Assistant's Guide to Effective Interaction: How to Maximise Your Practice*, Oxon: Routledge
13. Education Endowment Foundation (2014) *Press Release – Teaching Assistants can Improve Numeracy and Literacy when Used Effectively.* Retrieved from https://educationendowmentfoundation.org.uk/news/teaching-assistants-can-improve-numeracy-and-literacy-when-used-effectively
14. Charlie Henry, HMI, National Education Trust Annual SEND conference, 2013. Retrieved from http://www.nationaleducationtrust.net/Events/PastEvents/29_NETNovember2013.pdf
15. Professor Robert Coe, CEM. *Improving Education* (2013) Retrieved from http://www.cem.org/attachments/publications/ImprovingEducation2013.pdf
16. Ofsted. *Key Stage 3: The Wasted Years?* (2015). Retrieved from https://www.gov.uk/government/publications/key-stage-3-the-wasted-years
17. Kate Atkins, Headteacher Rosendale Primary School. *Why is meta-cognition Important in Schools?* (2014). Retrieved from http://www.reflectedlearning.org.uk/metacognition/
18. National Governors Association Guidance. *Pupil Premium.* Retrieved from www.nga.org.uk/Guidance/Holding-your-school-to-account/Premiums/Pupil-Premium-(1).aspx
19. Lillington School, Warwickshire. Retrieved from www.lillingtonschool.org
20. Raynham Primary School, Enfield. Retrieved from http://www.raynhamprimaryschool.co.uk/school/pupil-premium
21. The Downs Primary School, Essex. Retrieved from http://www.downs.essex.sch.uk/page/?title=Pupil+Premium&pid=19
22. Oakdene Primary School, Stockton on Tees. Retrieved from www.sbcschools.org.uk/oakdene.
23. Dr Tessa Stone. Closing the Gap Beyond the Classroom (2015) National Education Trust Pupil Premium Conference, Gloucester 2015. Retrieved from http://www.nationaleducationtrust.net/Events/PastEvents/78_NET.pdf

24. St Joseph's Catholic Primary School, Camden. Retrieved from *www.stjosephs.camden.sch.uk*
25. Tony Ashmore and Takako Yeung. *Counterblasts Pupil Premium* (2012). National Education Trust. Retrieved from http://www.amseducational.co.uk/freedownloads/counterblasts-premium-pupil.pdf
26. Seamus Oates, TBAP Trust. *Outstanding Use of the Pupil Premium Through Data Driven Inclusion*. Second Annual SEND Conference, National Education Trust. (2014). Retrieved from http://www.nationaleducationtrust.net/Events/PastEvents/59_SeamusOates.pdf
27. Katharine Dill, Robert J. Flynn, Matthew Hollingshead and Auriole Fernandes. *Children and Youth Services Review – Improving the Education Achievement of Young People in Out-of-Home Care* (pg 1081-1083) (2012)
28. Louis Cozolino. *The Social Neuroscience of Education* (2013)
29. Sir John Dunford, John Dunford Consulting. *Looked After Children Data* (2014)
30. Louise Bomber. *What About Me?* (2011)
31. Jean Domonique Bauby. *The Diving-Bell and the Butterfly* (2018)
32. Harper Lee. *To Kill a Mockingbird* (1960)
33. Phillip Pullman. *Clockwork* (2004)
34. Extracts from Ofsted Inspection Reports of Pupil Premium Award Winners 2014. Retrieved from www.ofsted.gov.uk
35. Théodre Géricault. *The Raft of the Medusa* (1819). The Louvre, Paris
36. Marc Rowland. *What Should I Spend my Pupil Premium on?* Schools Week (2015)
37. Ofsted. *Analysis and Challenge Tools for Schools* (2014). Retrieved from www.gov.uk/government/uploads/system/uploads/attachment_data/file/413824/The_Pupil_Premium_-_Analysis_and_challenge_tools_for_schools.doc